Saint Paul

HOME

FOR

ALL

SEASONS

SAINT PAUL

Saint Paul
HOME FOR ALL SEASONS

Introduction by Paul Molitor

Art Direction by Robert Shatzer

Sponsored by
The Saint Paul Area Chamber of Commerce

URBAN
TAPESTRY
SERIES
TOWERY
PUBLISHING, INC.

Contents

By Paul Molitor

Participating in baseball as a little kid in Minnesota tends to give a person a healthy dose of perspective. The summers are terrific—ideal weather for America's pastime. But every year there's that long, long winter to endure, with snow piled high on the diamonds, and with baseball bats and gloves stowed neatly in basement boxes.

There's a real upside to being a baseball player here, though: It gives you some-

thing to dream about during the off season, and thus it helps you get through our long winters.

Then the weather turns warm, and there's just something magic about those first couple of weeks of spring, when you get your glove out of the basement and convince your Dad to go out in the backyard with you to play catch. You start getting in shape, ready to try and make the team.

I recall those days fondly as one of the rites of spring that not only helped me get through the very cold winters up here as a kid, but that also have come to symbolize much that is good about Saint Paul. There was an

innocent, simple joy in the changing of the seasons, and it remains a poignant memory to this day.

Now that I've had 21 Major League seasons, and have returned to live here, I am relearning many of these simple pleasures. I'm constantly being reminded why Saint Paul is such a special place to work and to live.

Saint Paul was definitely a good place to be a kid, a good place to grow up. First of all, I loved it here just because of the safety of being able to go out of your house and run down the street or the alley to your friend's house, whether it was 8 o'clock in the morning or 8 o'clock at night, whether it was December or July. It was safe to just go and hang out with your friends.

More often than not, we'd hang out in one of the almost countless parks and playgrounds that dot the city. No matter what neighborhood you're in, there has always been a choice of several parks and playgrounds within walking distance or bike-riding distance. This gave us all a place to go, whether we participated in a sport or whether we just wanted to get on the merry-go-rounds and the swings and spin around until our heads swam.

I know that being a part of this environment—the parks and playgrounds, the small-town feel of the residential areas, the distinctive neighborhoods where we realized that everybody knew everybody else's name—has helped me throughout my life and my career in baseball. The small-town values, where people seemed intent on building real communities, were reinforced by the lessons that I learned on the diamond, lessons like how to deal with adversity, how to maintain self-esteem, how to be self-disciplined, how to stay focused under pressure. I think sports add to these values at every level, from sandlot games to the Major Leagues.

All of which comes to mind when I think of

growing up in Saint Paul. Now, I have chosen to return to become a part of a community that still cares very much about its young people.

Not everything, of course, remains the same. Not by a long shot. As with every big city, Saint Paul has done plenty of growing during the two decades I spent playing Major League baseball.

Through it all, the city has retained much of its character and has remained a city of high values. There are still lots of churches, lots of big families, plenty of kids around. When I was a kid, on our block we had at least eight families with eight or more kids, and some had as many as 16 children. I guess in that regard, at least, things probably have changed quite a bit. But I like to think that the values of the city, the niceness and the mind-set of its people, have remained in the face of this growth.

But today, Saint Paul shares much, both good and bad, with other big cities. There's been a considerable amount of growth in Saint Paul during the years I worked away from town. The skyline has changed, the business community has grown and prospered, and the city has continued to stretch its borders. There's been a great deal of development here, most notably with an increase in entrepreneurial opportunities. People have been encouraged to take advantage of private opportunities to open businesses, whether it's shops or restaurants, on some of the main streets throughout the city.

One very visible change in the cityscape is the recently opened Xcel Energy Center. The Center houses the new Minnesota Wild NHL

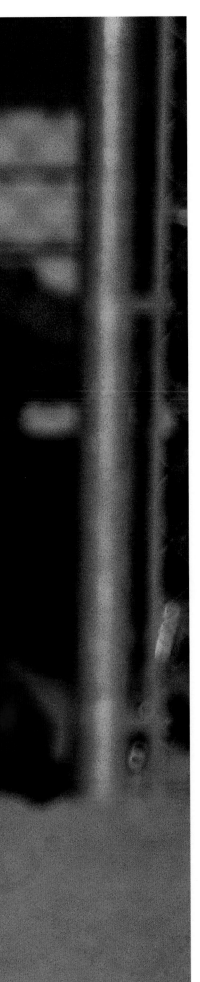

hockey team, bringing a major professional sport to Saint Paul. In addition to being proud of the team, Saint Paul is quite proud of this new, beautiful arena.

Another recent development: the tremendously impressive new Science Museum of Minnesota downtown. It's already entertained thousands and thousands of people, and is interactive as well as entertaining, with lots of hands-on exhibits. It's added to what the city already has to offer to young people.

And just the overall renaissance of the downtown area is important, the way it's cleaned up and made the city more attractive for families. The Ordway Center for the Performing Arts is just one example. It's where Broadway-quality plays and entertainment are bringing people back to downtown Saint Paul.

On the outside the changes are numerous, and very visible. The new buildings, the renovations, and the refurbished neighborhoods—all stand out as signs of progress.

But on the inside, I don't think the city has changed at all in one very important aspect of its character. Despite its growth, Saint Paul has a very nicely paced lifestyle. Things are measured—not too frantic, not too laid-back—creating a

really nice blend of the progressive and the conservative. I've maintained the friendships from high school and university that I had growing up here. We've all grown and changed, just as the city has, but we've all somehow managed to fashion our lives according to the wonderful rhythm and pace of the city.

I've learned a lot more about Saint Paul, and the surrounding area in the Midwest, through the Molitor Fields for Kids Program. In 1998, when I was ending my playing career, the Twins came to me and asked me if I'd be interested in lending my name and

SAINT PAUL

support to this project, which is devoted to renovating old baseball fields throughout the Midwest. Naturally, I was very flattered. The Twins thought that it would be nice for me not only as a hometown guy, but as a tribute to some of the things that I've tried to contribute to as a player, by encouraging baseball and softball for boys and girls of all backgrounds.

Through various sponsorships and grants—and of course through the Twins organization—we have, to date, renovated some 70 fields, at a cost of about $5,000 per field. So, we've invested about $350,000 thus far, with more on the way. I've been fortunate enough to go to a lot of the dedications, and I'm really impressed not only by the aesthetic beauty of the renovations but also by the communities' backing of this project. It's been a great program and I'm anxious to continue to develop it.

There's something about how the look of a well-maintained baseball field adds to the atmosphere of the game and makes kids want to get out there and participate. Whether it's Little League baseball or girl's softball, there's definitely a difference in how a good field changes the whole feeling of the game.

On a summer night, when you turn the lights on; or on a Saturday morning when you can see the grass still wet from the dew: It's really magic. And it's really made a difference for me to see how the communities have come together to take care of these fields and give the kids some of the magic of the game.

There's one particular field in Saint Paul—Midway Stadium, home of the minor league Saint Paul Saints baseball team—that is the site of a particularly interesting kind of magic. Here you have perhaps the most interesting and successful minor league team in the

country. The ownership has done an outstanding job of promoting the team, so much so that there have been times over the past few years when the Saints have outdrawn the Twins (in Minneapolis) during a given home stand. Midway's got everything from a picnic area in left field where you can sit and have a little bit different view of the ball game to massages done by nuns at the game. Bill Murray has been part of the ownership team, and that ought to tell you something right there. The fact that it's outdoors, whereas the Twins are indoors, has made a difference, and it's been a tremendously successful minor league franchise and a big part of baseball here in Minnesota.

Baseball is not, despite my career, the only thing I notice. I enjoy the fact that Saint Paul offers something unique or exciting or edifying—or all three at once. Saint Paul is a city that knows how to have fun, but it's also a city that cares about its cultural life, from the highbrow to the down-home. The following are just a few of my favorites:

The Minnesota State Fair, which runs from late August through Labor Day, is certainly a big part of Minnesota's heritage and tradition. The various midway rides, the competitions, and the shows—it's a huge attraction, and signals the change of the season from summer to what's usually a really beautiful autumn.

When it gets really, really cold, the Saint Paul Winter Carnival gets heated up. This is a big extravaganza, a tremendous festival that includes everything from a treasure hunt with clues every day in the newspaper to an ice sculpture contest. There's no doubt that the Winter Carnival brings lots of warmth to lots of people during our tough Minnesota winters. ➤

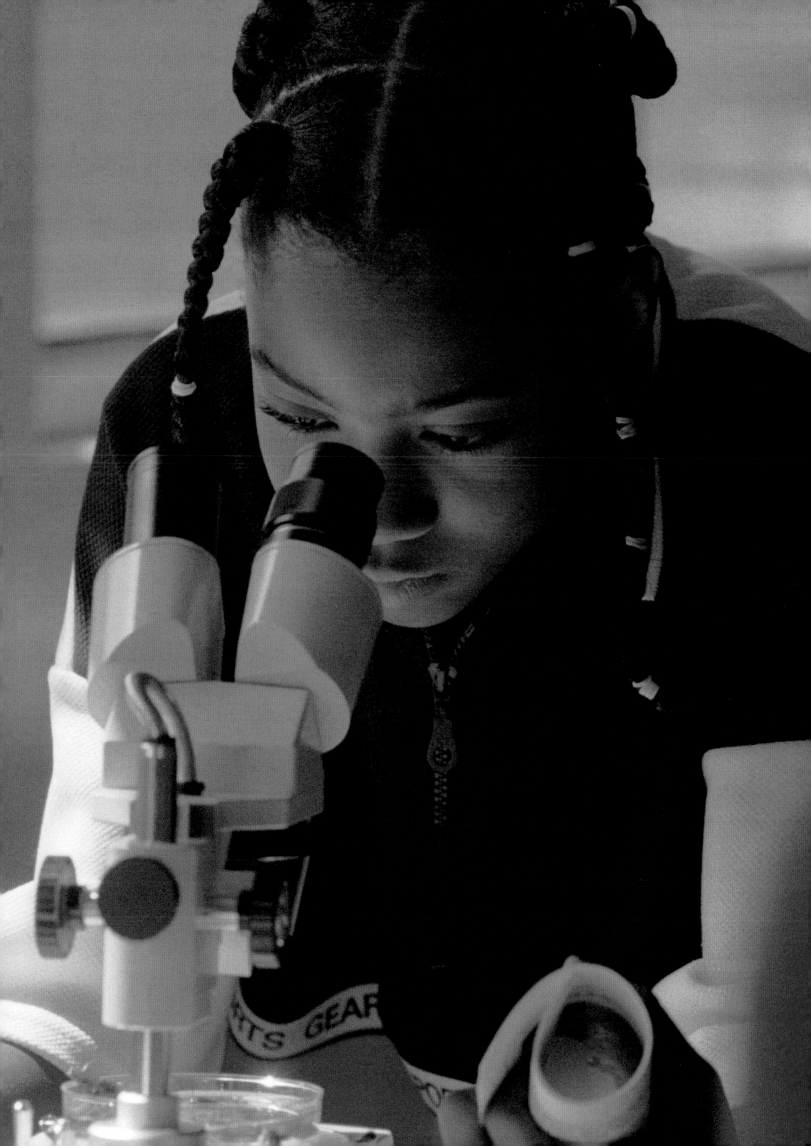

SAINT PAUL

In the summertime, Grand Old Day is a one-day festival that attracts about 250,000 people to Grand Avenue, a street that runs through the heart of Saint Paul. It highlights all the activity that the street has throughout the year, which is very eclectic, with outdoor shops and restaurants and cafés. There's a parade, and a 10K race, live music, and an all-day street festival that runs along a five-mile stretch of Grand Avenue from downtown to the river.

And finally, a sentimental favorite: the paths along the Mississippi River. These paths are especially beautiful in Saint Paul, particularly in the fall when the color changes. There's nothing like a bike ride down the River on a nice September afternoon. You can extend that ride by taking a turn east and going down Summit Avenue, a wide boulevard that runs through beautiful trees and historic mansions. One in particular is the Governor's Mansion about halfway down between River Boulevard and downtown Saint Paul.

Any season of the year, Saint Paul is a terrific place. But for me, it's especially nice in the early spring, when my thoughts always seem to wander back to those days when I'd go down to the basement, find my baseball glove in one of the boxes, and go outside to test the air to see if it was warm and fresh enough for a game of catch. That's when I recognize the feel of the place the best, the feel of a place called home. ■

ITTING ALONG THE NORTHEAST
banks of the Mississippi River,
Saint Paul was once known as the
Last City in the East. Today, it is a
center of government, serving as
both the seat of Ramsey County
and the capital of Minnesota.

GUESTS AT THE HISTORIC
Saint Paul Hotel (LEFT)—
built by local businessman Lucius
P. Ordway and opened in 1910—will
find themselves at the heart of
the city's activity. Within walking
distance stands the Minnesota
World Trade Center (OPPOSITE),
a business complex complete with
a 52-foot fountain.

SAINT PAUL

LOCKED INDOORS BY Minnesota's snowy winters, locals capitalize on outside gatherings during Saint Paul's near-perfect summer months. Downtown spaces—such as Rice Park's fountain (TOP)—become meeting places for business and pleasure.

PUBLIC ART FLOURISHES throughout downtown, mingling with high-rises that are compelling works of art in their own right. An art deco landmark, the 20-story Saint Paul City Hall and Ramsey County Courthouse (LEFT) is the only skyscraper in the country to house a city hall. Showcasing a more corporate style of architecture, Ecolab Center (OPPOSITE) is world head-quarters of the cleaning supplies giant after which it is named.

S AINT PAUL'S LEGACY COMES alive in the facades of its buildings, including the headquarters of the St. Paul Companies (TOP LEFT), the oldest company in the state; Regions Hospital (BOTTOM), originally established in 1872; and the First National Bank Building (OPPOSITE), whose trademark neon sign punctuates the city's skyline. Tracing the state's past through hundreds of years, the Minnesota History Center (TOP RIGHT) houses various exhibits and archives of the Minnesota Historical Society.

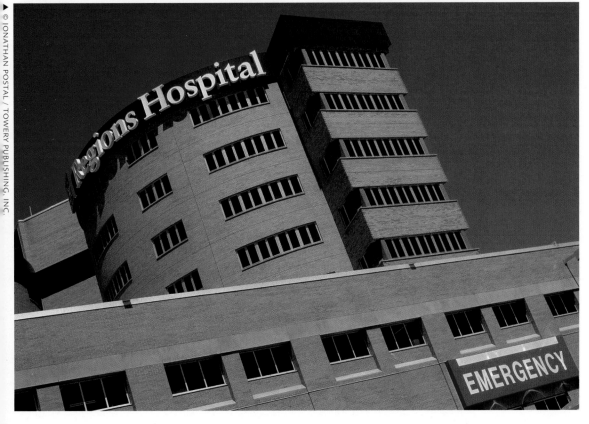

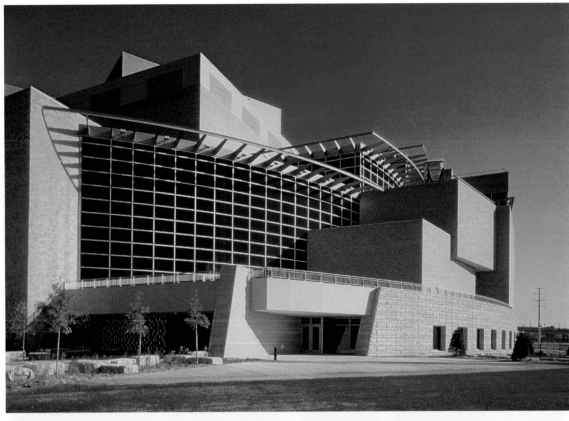

ACH YEAR, THOUSANDS OF
residents and visitors have a
ball in downtown Saint Paul. The
Minnesota Children's Museum
(BOTTOM LEFT) and the Science
Museum of Minnesota (TOP) inspire
curiosity in all who participate in
their interactive exhibits. Shoppers
seeking a unique, outdoor retail
environment flock to the city's
Seventh Place Mall (BOTTOM RIGHT).

T HE SKY'S THE LIMIT: WHETHER to enhance atmosphere or to provide sunlight for foliage, many of Saint Paul's buildings combine the natural with the urban in their spacious interiors.

MANY OF DOWNTOWN Saint Paul's buildings reflect the city's economic and business activity. But Como Park Conservatory (TOP) showcases the area's commitment to horticulture. Opened in 1915 and listed on the National Register of Historic Places, the facility features seasonal and permanent exhibits of flowers and plants, and hosts several parties, concerts, and weddings each year.

Upper
Mississippi
River
Navigation
Charts

US Army Corps
of Engineers

1999

Cities of Mississippi
Nineteenth Development

John W. Reps

S AINT PAUL'S RESIDENTS are known for their innovation and—in the case of 3M corporate scientist and Post-It Note inventor Arthur Fry (BOTTOM RIGHT)—their stick-to-itiveness. Enlivening the city with color and style, artist Tacoumba Aiken (BOTTOM LEFT) has exhibited his work nationwide. Real estate developer Jerry Trooien (TOP), head of the JLT Group, Inc., has developed much of the land along the Mississippi River, while Tom Welna (OPPOSITE) operates Covington Inn, a popular bed-and-breakfast housed in a 1940s tugboat that floats on the river's waters.

ON SUNNY SUMMER DAYS, Minnesota's lakes swarm with windsurfers, wakeboarders, and skiers riding the waves. Throughout the warm months, Captain William D. Bowell Sr. (OPPOSITE), founder and owner of Padelford Packet Boat Co., Inc., and his crew lead riverboat tours of the Mississippi River, narrating Saint Paul's history along the way.

WITH THE LUSH LANDSCAPES of its public buildings, Saint Paul is awash in scenic splendor. But some locals opt for the backyard variety of fountains of youth—preferably accompanied by equal amounts of delight and squealing.

MINNESOTA HONORS ITS heroes through numerous memorials on the grounds of the state capitol. The Minnesota Peace Officer Memorial (TOP) commemorates the men and women who lost their lives in the line of duty, while the Roy Wilkins Memorial (BOTTOM LEFT AND RIGHT) remembers the local civil rights leader with 46 bronze sculptures. An eight-foot bronze infantryman and an 18-foot bronze column comprise the Minnesota Korean War Veterans Memorial (OPPOSITE), which was dedicated in 1998.

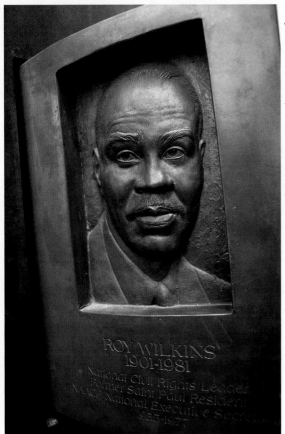

© JONATHAN POSTAL / TOWERY PUBLISHING, INC.

THIS SIDE OF PARADISE: Named for U.S. Senator Henry M. Rice, Rice Park (BOTTOM LEFT AND RIGHT) is the scene of scores of picnics and lunch breaks every day. Adjacent to the park, the Landmark Center (TOP)—formerly known as the Federal Court House building—houses the Minnesota Museum of American Art and the Schubert Club Piano Museum. Greeting visitors to the facility is a bronze statue of Saint Paul native F. Scott Fitzgerald (OPPOSITE), who wrote such literary masterpieces as *Tender Is the Night* and *The Great Gatsby*.

IT'S ACADEMIC: ALWAYS CAUSE for celebration, graduation from one of Saint Paul's excellent private colleges gets students going in the right direction. Macalester College (LEFT), the University of Saint Thomas (OPPOSITE TOP), and the College of Saint Catherine (OPPOSITE BOTTOM) are all renowned for their quality programs.

SAINT PAUL

SAINT PAUL'S LOOMING BUILD-ings aren't the only structures that reach for the sky. Erected in Ecolab Plaza and unveiled in 2000, *Skygate* (TOP)—a public sculpture designed by R.M. Fischer—rises more than 50 feet in the air. KSTP-TV (OPPOSITE) has reached new heights of a different kind: The first television station in the Midwest, KSTP is today the only one in the Twin Cities that is still locally owned and operated.

ORNERING A CHUNK OF the insurance market in the Midwest, Minnesota Life (LEFT) provides some $209 billion in coverage to more than 6 million clients throughout the country. Minnesota Public Radio broadcasts from nearly 30 stations throughout the region, including KNOW FM 91.1 and KSJN FM 99.5 (OPPOSITE), the Twin Cities' most popular classical music station.

DOWNTOWN SAINT PAUL HAS become one big hard-hat area, with ongoing construction marking the city's continuing expansion. New retail spaces and office buildings—such as the Lawson Commons complex (OPPOSITE)—are not only boosting the local economy, but also changing the face of the city.

S AINT PAUL HAS TRULY GONE
wild for the Xcel Energy Center,
home of the NHL Minnesota Wild
hockey team, as well as numerous
amateur and high school sports
events. The arena is part of the
extensive RiverCentre complex,
which also houses the Touchstone
Energy Plaza, a state-of-the-art
convention facility, and the Roy
Wilkins Auditorium, which hosts
concerts and traveling exhibits.

SAINT PAUL

S AINT PAUL'S GROWTH IS NOT merely economic in nature, but spiritual as well. Opportunities abound for locals to get involved with churches and synagogues throughout the region, while some residents—regardless of age—prefer the personal meditation available through walking labyrinths.

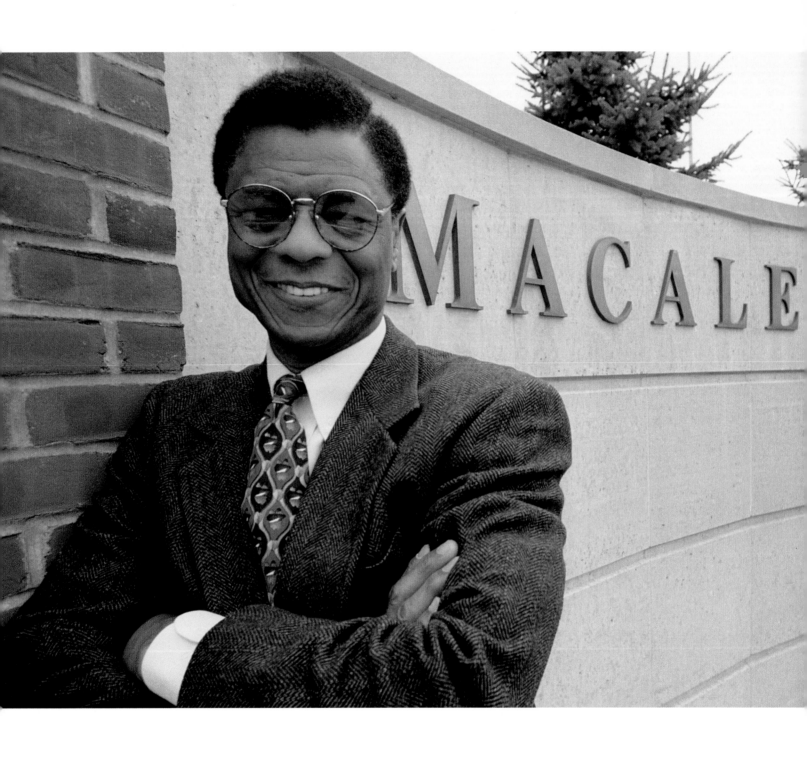

Saint Paul's historic buildings can demand a great deal of work and attention to keep them in tip-top condition. Keeping students at Macalester College in shape is the job of Irv Cross (OPPOSITE), a former NFL player and CBS commentator who now serves as the school's athletic director.

From any angle, the Minnesota State Capitol is an awe-inspiring sight. The building, designed by local architect Cass Gilbert, is topped with one of the largest unsupported marble domes in the world. Standing in sharp contrast to the building's monochromatic exterior, four gilded statues—representing Civilization, Nature, Prosperity, and Minnesota—oversee the decisions made within.

SINCE IT WAS OPENED IN 1905, the Minnesota State Capitol building has seen many sessions of political activity under its roof. At the helm of the capital city's burgeoning renaissance is Mayor Norm Coleman (OPPOSITE), who has, since taking office in 1993, helped to secure a National Hockey League team—the Minnesota Wild—and to open the Science Museum of Minnesota.

ROM KITSCHY NOSTALGIA TO religious faith, from Power-Books to the Good Book, Saint Paulites hold many things very dear to them. Seaneen Brennan (LEFT) owns and operates East End Funky Stuff, an antique store filled with relics of pop cultures past. A mechanical engineer, Patrick Ferrin (OPPOSITE TOP) has gone to great lengths to use his Macintosh PowerBook instead of a PC to draft diagrams, claiming his computer can save the state both time and money. Focusing on souls instead of cents are Father Bob Hart at the Cathedral of Saint Paul (OPPOSITE, BOTTOM LEFT) and Rabbi Jonathan H. Ginsburg at Temple of Aaron (OPPOSITE, BOTTOM RIGHT).

SAINT PAUL

Situated on the highest point in the city, the Cathedral of Saint Paul draws congregation members as well as tourists to view its Classical Renaissance-style exterior and resplendently ornate interior. Opened in 1915 and consecrated in 1958, the 3,000-seat cathedral today serves as the Mother Church of the Archdiocese of Saint Paul and Minneapolis.

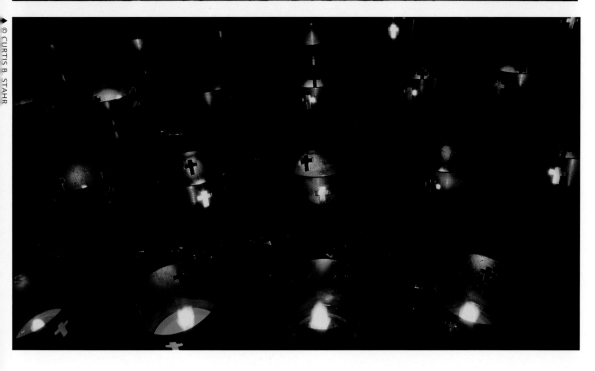

The Cathedral of Saint Paul honors numerous Catholic saints—including its namesake patron—through the intricately designed and richly colored stained-glass windows that grace its walls.

MINNESOTA OFFERS A UNIQUE window of opportunity for local music enthusiasts. In celebration of the state's contributions to popular song, Mike McColl, Benjamin Filene, and Patrick Grace (BOTTOM, FROM LEFT) organized *Sounds Good to Me: Music in Minnesota* at the Minnesota History Center. As copastor of the youth-oriented House of Mercy, Russell Rathbun (TOP) adds "hymns" by performers like Johnny Cash, Hank Williams, and Violent Femmes to the church's nontraditional services.

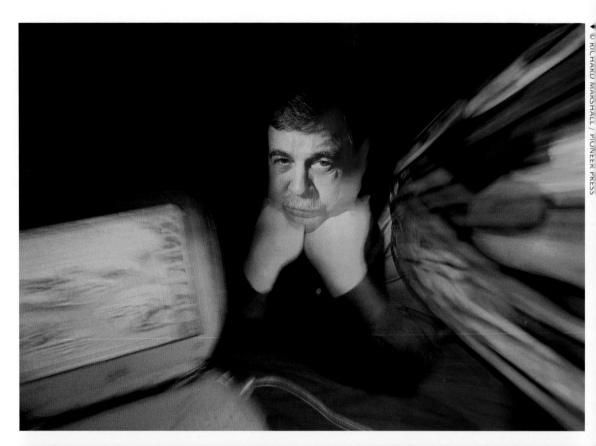

While Rae van Wyhe (LEFT), director of the Minnesota Tourism Office, beckons travelers to explore the state's many attractions, John Risdall (OPPOSITE TOP), chairman and CEO of Risdall Linnihan Advertising Interactive, promotes several Minnesota businesses through high-tech campaigns. Essaying the advantages of Macintosh computers, Saint Paul native Rodney O. Lain (OPPOSITE BOTTOM) contributes regular columns to a number of on-line publications, including *MacAddict* and *TheiMac*.

THROUGH A NUMBER OF health care centers and research facilities, Saint Paul strives to protect its children and treat their illnesses effectively and compassionately. As director of trauma services at Regions Hospital, Michael D. McGonigal, M.D. (LEFT) campaigns against gun violence through programs like Calling the Shots. Under the supervision of Medical Director Fatih Uckun, M.D. (OPPOSITE, ON LEFT), the Parker Hughes Cancer Center treats cancer and leukemia patients with state-of-the-art, personalized care.

E ACH YEAR, VISITORS BY THE trainload choo-choose to visit Saint Paul's Twin Cities Model Railroad Museum. The organization relies on volunteers and engineers such as Ray Norton (OPPOSITE) for its innovative, year-round displays, including *Trains at Bandana* (ABOVE), an exhibit devoted to American railroading from the 1930s through the 1950s.

A FORMER RAILROAD REPAIR shop, Bandana Square (TOP) is back on track as a popular retail center, attracting thousands of shoppers to its stores and restaurants. The railroad's influence on Saint Paul's history and economy gives many residents the [loco]motive to indulge their train interests.

F OR MORE THAN 50 YEARS, Mickey's Dining Car has offered Saint Paulites a little taste of history. The 1937 O'Mahoney railcar is listed on the National Register of Historic Places, but more important, it has many regulars who frequent the establishment on a daily basis.

SAINT PAUL

M USIC AFFECTS ALL SAINT
Paulites, regardless of race,
age, or even species. Conducted by
Eiji Oue (TOP), the Minnesota
Orchestra gives some 200 concerts
a year, and the Saint Paul Civic
Symphony (BOTTOM RIGHT) and
Minnesota Youth Symphony
(BOTTOM LEFT) attract a fair share
of local listeners as well. To better
reflect the city's expanding arts
scene, the former Ordway Music
Theatre changed its name to the
Ordway Center for the Performing
Arts (OPPOSITE TOP) in January
2000. On hand at the official
ceremony were Saint Paul Mayor
Norm Coleman and Ordway Presi-
dent and CEO Kevin McCollum
(OPPOSITE BOTTOM, FROM LEFT).

ALL SAINT PAUL'S A STAGE, AND the men and women merely players—albeit very talented ones with many opportunities to display their craft. Established in 1963, the Minnesota Opera (TOP) performs the works of Puccini, Mozart, and others at the Ordway Center for the Performing Arts (OPPOSITE). Founded by Lou Bellamy (BOTTOM LEFT), the Penumbra Theatre Company stages the works of African-American playwrights, many of whom have gone on to national prominence. The SteppingStone Theatre—with Richard Hitchler (BOTTOM RIGHT) acting as artistic director—gives children and teenagers a chance to get in on the action.

S AINT PAUL'S EASTERN CULTURE comes to life in the colorful performances of the Chinese American Association of Minnesota Chinese Dance Theater. In addition to its many shows each year—some featuring the work of choreographer Shen Pei (OPPOSITE CENTER)—the group operates a dance school and sponsors outreach programs around the city.

The city's many cultures—represented by strong Hispanic, Native American, European, and Middle Eastern populations—create a kaleidoscope of color in Saint Paul, as residents proudly celebrate their heritages through public gatherings and festivities.

Saint Paul's diverse cultural makeup translates into a feast of foods from around the world. El Burrito Mercado, owned and operated by Mary and Tomas Silva (BOTTOM RIGHT), ranks as one of the oldest Mexican groceries in the city; Ari and Cassandra Apostolou's Acropol Inn (OPPOSITE, TOP LEFT) lays claim to being the area's first Greek eatery. Tanya Fuad and Rodwan Nakshabandi (OPPOSITE, BOTTOM LEFT) opened Babani's, the first Kurdish restaurant in the country, in 1997. At Big Daddy's Old Kentucky Barbeque, owner and chef Gene "Big Daddy" Sampson (LEFT) served up home-cooked dishes until the diner closed in December 2000. A more recent addition to the Saint Paul restaurant scene, Bertil's, owned and operated by siblings Bert and Melissa Mattson (TOP RIGHT), opened in May 2000 and specializes in upscale dining.

AT THE ST. PAUL FARMERS'
Market, area growers gather
to sell a cornucopia of fresh produce, cheeses, meats, syrups, and
baked goods. Established a year
before Saint Paul was incorporated in 1854, the market attracts
thousands of visitors and more
than 150 farmers each week.

LEND AN EAR: SOME 200,000 Minnesotans live on farms, harvesting crops that are shipped throughout the country. But even with so many healthy veggies in the area, many still prefer a mustard-slathered corn dog at the Minnesota State Fair.

Each year, more than 1.5 million people attend the Minnesota State Fair—one of the largest in the United States—to play games, shop at the many booths selling crafts and clothes, and sample the more than 500 kinds of food. One of the fair's most popular delicacies has been the Pronto Pup—some 500,000 are sold there each year.

SAINT PAUL

AN AIR OF FESTIVITY AND FUN
pervades the Mighty Midway
at the Minnesota State Fair, as
visitors ride the waves in bumper
boats and soar through the air on
roller coasters.

HELD DURING THE FIRST WEEKS of summer, the Grand Old Day (BOTTOM) is truly fit for the King: It is one of the Midwest's largest one-day festivals, attracting some 250,000 fans. While it draws fewer attendees, the Flying Colors Kite Festival (OPPOSITE) nevertheless sets spirits soaring. Another Minnesota high flyer, Charles A. Lindbergh—who made the first nonstop flight across the Atlantic Ocean—is remembered with a pair of statues near the state capitol (TOP).

LOCATED A FEW MILES SOUTH-west of downtown Saint Paul, the Minneapolis-St. Paul International Airport is really taking off. Approximately 30 million travelers pass through its gates each year, and with that number expected to grow steadily, the airport is undergoing a long-term, $2.6 billion renovation plan—slated for completion in 2010—to modernize and expand its facilities and services.

SAINT PAUL

CALLING SAINT PAUL FAMILY friendly isn't just blowing hot air. The city's protective environment and limitless opportunities lift it high above many other urban areas.

At the heart of Saint Paul's appeal lie its neighborhoods. Majestic mansions and cozy porches line the streets, as do whimsical statues carved from the salvaged trunks of the area's beloved elm trees—lost to disease, but not forgotten.

I MPRESSIVE ON A GRAND SCALE as well as in its finely wrought details, the James J. Hill House was the largest and most expensive home in the Midwest when it was completed in 1891. Hill, a railroad magnate who co-owned the Great Northern Railroad company, oversaw the construction of the five-story structure, including the installation of 16 crystal chandeliers, more than 20 fireplaces, and the two-story art gallery.

GARRISON KEILLOR ONCE referred to his fellow Minnesotans as "God's frozen people," and it's easy to see why: The state gets more than 46 inches of snow per year. But the accumulation results in quite a beautiful blanket, from the burbs all the way to the governor's mansion on Summit Avenue (TOP).

MINNESOTA'S COLD WINTERS don't stand in the way of growth, at least not when it comes to housing development. The building trades boast a history as old as Saint Paul's. When the city's first business directory was published in 1850, a listing of 18 carpenters outnumbered listings for all the other occupational groups.

SAINT PAUL

Each January, Saint Paul's popular Winter Carnival pays tribute to the season. The festival, first held in 1886, celebrated its centennial in 1986 with a massive castle made from hun-dreds of blocks of ice (ABOVE). Today, the event features a full schedule of winter sports, games, parades, and—in what is truly a winter wanderland—an elaborate ice maze (OPPOSITE).

T HE ALLURE OF SNOW BRINGS out the playful nature of Saint Paul's residents—young, old, and even animal (PAGES 124-129).

SAINT PAUL

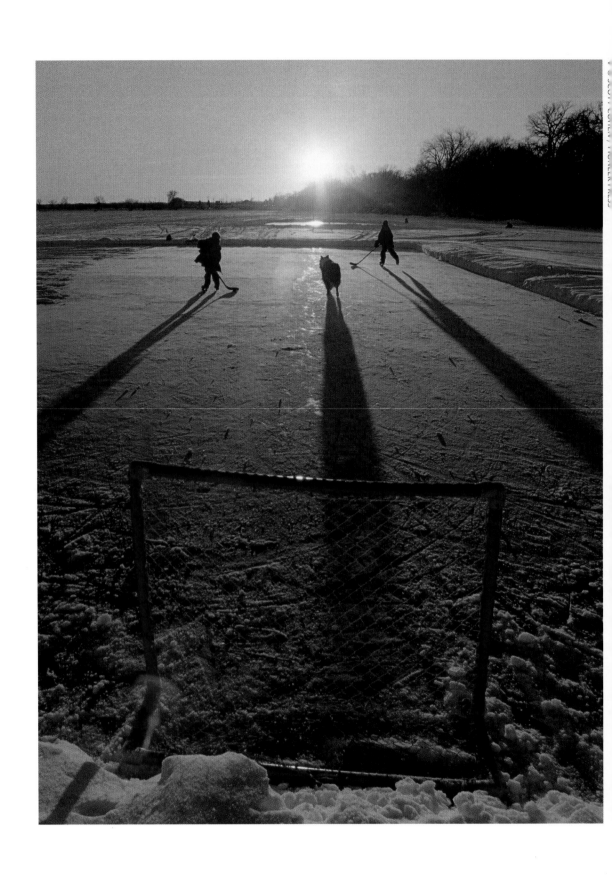

I n Minnesota, hockey is more than just a sport. For many enthusiasts, rinks, pucks, hat tricks, and hip checks constitute a way of life. Toward this goal, children and teenagers have many opportunities to participate in school teams and organized leagues—or simply to play an early-morning pickup game on a frozen lake.

STARTING OUT WITH A BANG: On September 29, 2000, the state's new National Hockey League franchise, the Minnesota Wild, played its first preseason home game in Saint Paul, marking the inaugural event at the Xcel Energy Center. More than 18,000 fans watched as the home team scored a 3-1 victory over the Anaheim Mighty Ducks.

B EING ACTIVE IN SAINT PAUL sports—whether individually or as part of an organized team— means gritting your teeth, getting a grip, and giving it your all.

THE COMPETITIVE SPIRIT motivates scores of young athletes in Minnesota. While many of them get in the ring to compete individually, more youths than ever are participating in team sports at the high school level.

SINCE 1993, THE SAINT PAUL Saints have been a near-constant presence at the top of the Northern League standings, as well as a consistent draw for minor league baseball fans around the region. The 2000 season marked the team's sixth year with first-base coach Wayne Terwilliger (TOP)—and his 51st year in professional baseball.

Boyz on the hood: Saint Paul goes wild for racing cars and stars, especially during the annual Miller Lite 300. Held during the Minnesota State Fair, the event features a pack of big-name drivers, including Mike Garvey (OPPOSITE), who took the checkered flag in 1999.

MOBILITY COMES IN MANY forms. Attendees at the Minnesota State Fair take in Old Ruthie (OPPOSITE TOP), a Model A jalopy adorned with an odd assortment of artifacts. But for most locals, getting around town under your own power tops the list of options.

FORD

- 1954 -
MINNESOTA
748-122
COLLECTOR
FORD

GRILLS AND THRILLS: HOT RODS and vintage cars still cruise the strip along University Avenue, as they did during the 1950s and 1960s. A popular hangout then and now, the red-and-white-checked Porky's opened in 1953 and today stands as one of the city's last authentic drive-ins.

S TARRY-EYED CHILDREN TOUR
the merry displays of Christmas

Each December, as Saint Paul gets into the Christmas spirit, it's common to see yards and houses aglow with a host of festive holiday decorations, including 12 drummers drumming, 11 pipers piping, 10 lords a-leaping, nine ladies dancing....

THE TORCHLIGHT PARADES (CENTER) march through Saint Paul, marking the closing days of the annual Winter Carnival. Fireworks provide a fitting finale, but many onlookers prefer the ice-works created by local sculptors.

SAINT PAUL

AS IF FREEZING TEMPERATURES and snow flurries weren't enough, Saint Paul's Winter Carnival also involves frozen treats and big blocks of ice. In 1999, Twin Cities-based Kemp's Marigold Foods debuted the festival's official ice cream, a flavor called Zero Visibility, at a tasting in Rice Park, where Governor Jesse Ventura (OPPOSITE BOTTOM) enjoyed the treat with other celebrants. During the 2000 festival, ice sculptors created a tribute in Rice Park to *Peanuts* creator and Saint Paul native Charles Schulz.

I n Saint Paul, ice is an integral part of the landscape, and
residents make the most of it by
sculpting fanciful figures from
frozen water.

THE CITY HAS CARVED AN impressive niche for itself in the Midwest, and the unique spirit and personality of its population make Saint Paul truly a home for all seasons.

Profiles in Excellence

A look at the corporations, businesses, professional groups, and community service organizations that have made this book possible. Their stories—offering an informal chronicle of the local business community—are arranged according to the date they were established in the Saint Paul area.

3M ❖ Aero Systems Engineering, Inc.

Andersen Corporation ❖ AT&T

Bethel College & Seminary ❖ Bluestem Systems, Inc.

The Burlington Northern and Santa Fe Railway Company ❖ CBR Incorporated

Connecting Images, Inc. ❖ Convent of the Visitation School

Ecolab ❖ Ellerbe Becket

Embassy Suites Saint Paul ❖ Ericksen Ellison and Associates Inc.

Flannery Construction ❖ Fortis

James J. Hill Group ❖ KMSP-TV Channel 9

Larson·King, LLP ❖ Lawson Software

Lethert, Skwira, Schultz, & Co. LLP ❖ Long Cheng, Inc.

Metro Commuter Services ❖ Metropolitan State University

Minnesota Life ❖ National Checking Company

New Mech Companies, Inc. ❖ Northwest Airlines

NRG Energy, Inc. ❖ Ordway Center for the Performing Arts

Regions Hospital ❖ Ristorante Luci and Luci Ancora

Saint Paul Area Chamber of Commerce ❖ The St. Paul Companies, Inc.

Schreiber Mullaney Construction Co. Inc. ❖ Shavlik Technologies

Sitma USA, Inc. ❖ Summit Brewing Company

Sun Country Airlines ❖ Toltz, King, Duvall, Anderson & Associates, Inc.

United Hospital ❖ The Wabasha Street Caves

Wells Fargo & Company ❖ West Group ❖ Xcel Energy, Inc.

1850-1920

THE ST. PAUL COMPANIES, INC.

FOR NEARLY 150 YEARS, THE ST. PAUL COMPANIES, INC. HAS SERVED ST. PAUL both as an insurance company faithfully protecting its policyholders and as a good corporate citizen supporting its employees and enhancing the community. "There has always been the spirit of being part of the community and the need to give back to the community,"

says Karen Himle, senior vice president, corporate affairs. "Our success is closely linked to that of the community. It's where we live and work, where our employees are raised and educated."

The oldest business corporation in Minnesota, The St. Paul was founded in 1853 as St. Paul Fire and Marine Insurance Company. Its mission was to provide a Minnesota-based source of insurance for businesses and residents, who previously had to do business with faraway, East Coast insurers.

Since its creation, The St. Paul has quietly built a reputation of trust by developing insurance products to solve specific—and often urgent—needs. It has long been known as the dollar-for-dollar company that faithfully paid its claims based on full policy value— from the Great Chicago Fire of 1871 to the hurricanes of today. The St. Paul has grown, largely because of its excellent reputation, into one of the largest commercial property-liability insurers in the world.

Today, The St. Paul is a group of companies providing commercial property-liability insurance, life insurance, and nonlife reinsur-

ance products and services worldwide. In commercial insurance, The St. Paul focuses on specialized underwriting for individual industries and professions. For example, the firm is the leading medical liability insurer and top surety bond underwriter in the United States. Other commercial specialties include insurance for high-tech firms, financial institutions, municipalities, and lawyers, accountants, and other professionals.

THE ST. PAUL COMPANIES, INC. CORPORATE HEADQUARTERS IN DOWNTOWN ST. PAUL INCLUDES THE SOUTH BUILDING (LOWER RIGHT) AND THE PYRAMID-TOPPED NORTH BUILDING.

A GOOD PLACE TO WORK

Today, some 12,000 employees work for The St. Paul in 19 countries. It has been widely recognized for its farsighted stance on many workplace issues. "At every St. Paul Companies location, we have a strong commitment to our employees," says Himle. "It's part of The St. Paul's vision, which is to be known by our customers as a leading global provider of value-added insurance products and services; by our shareholders as a superior, long-term investment; and by our employees as an exceptional place to work."

At the company's downtown St. Paul headquarters, employees have access to a variety of amenities. A child care center accommodates 100 preschool-aged children and infants of employees. An employee fitness center offers a full range of workout equipment, health and fitness information, and aerobics and other classes. Even the smaller touches—special features in the employee cafeteria, for example, and a club that organizes employee social events—contribute to a high-quality work environment.

Recognizing the benefits of art in the workplace, the company displays pieces by world-renowned

BESIDES INVESTING 2 PERCENT OF YEARLY EARNINGS IN LOCAL COMMUNITIES, THE ST. PAUL'S COMMUNITY INVOLVEMENT INCLUDES SUBSTANTIAL EMPLOYEE VOLUNTEERISM.

JEFFREY GROSSCUP

artists throughout the bright, airy corridors of the headquarters building. The company also recognizes its employee artists with a biennial art show.

A Good Place to Live

Being a responsible corporate citizen involves more than being responsive to shareholders and employees; it also means acknowledging the company's responsibility to the larger community. The St. Paul donates 2 percent of its yearly earnings to local organizations involved in education, arts and culture, and community development.

"We want to do what we can to create opportunities for people and to build the capacity of communities to meet the challenges of a changing society," says Himle. The St. Paul has helped fund such programs as a local college initiative to attract minority students to careers in teaching, various neighborhood housing and business development projects, and a unique partnership to create activities to expose people to diversity issues through the arts.

But The St. Paul donates more than just money, according to Himle. "Our leadership and our employees are personally involved in community activities," she says. For example, more than 150 employees are involved locally in finding and securing grants for nonprofit organizations in their communities.

Nonprofit board involvement is strongly encouraged by the company, with many senior-level executives taking on significantly accountable positions in such groups. In addition, surveys have shown that the percentage of St. Paul Companies employees who volunteer in their communities is much higher than national averages.

Beyond encouraging employees to lead and volunteer for ongoing programs ranging from construction projects with Habitat for Humanity to mentor programs to Junior Achievement, St. Paul employees can have their personal charitable contributions matched by the company. More than one-fourth of employees—a very high percentage compared with other companies—participate in this program. Many employees sign up each fall for the company's charitable fund drive, in which donations to community service organizations such as United Way are deducted directly from an employee's paycheck.

The St. Paul believes that success can be achieved when shareholders, employees, and the community are all taken into account. "As stewards of shareholder assets, it is our duty to optimize the use of those assets," Himle says. "We do this by directing charitable resources in a way that realizes the benefits to comunity involvement. We also support opportunities for employees to grow and develop through community service, whether through opportunities they find for themselves or through company-organized volunteer programs. Through its support of people and institutions, The St. Paul hopes to create strong, healthy, vital communities."

Clockwise from top:
The St. Paul's headquarters reflects the character of a 21st-century company, whose traditions extend back to its founding in 1853.

From the trading room, employees of The St. Paul's investment division manage one of the strongest portfolios in the property-casualty insurance industry.

The company's downtown St. Paul headquarters offers a variety of employee amenities, including a fitness center.

Employees on the skyway connecting the north and south buildings of the St. Paul's headquarters look westward on Sixth Street.

JEFFREY GROSSCUP

JEFFREY GROSSCUP

THE BURLINGTON NORTHERN AND SANTA FE RAILWAY COMPANY

*I*N THE 1800S, WELL BEFORE THE FIRST CARS OR AIRPLANES, RAILROADS dominated the American landscape. Cities grew up around the rails, and the railroads blossomed. The tracks brought new industries to town, enhanced trade, and created opportunities that made people want to settle in the area. The Burlington Northern and Santa Fe Railway

Company (BNSF) has just such a rich history in St. Paul.

Today's BNSF was created through a series of mergers with other railroads, but its legacy in St. Paul began nearly 150 years ago with 10 miles of track between St. Paul and Minneapolis. With those first 10 miles built in 1862 by the St. Paul & Pacific Railway—what would later become industrialist James J. Hill's Great Northern Railway—the state of Minnesota entered the industrial age. Hill, known as The Empire Builder, extended his railroad west, completing a transcontinental main line from St. Paul to Seattle in 1893. Hill and the Great Northern brought new industries and agriculture to the region, as well as immigrants from Ireland and Germany.

The Northern Pacific, the other railroad that helped develop Minnesota, was created by an act of Congress signed by President Abraham Lincoln in 1864. The railway broke ground in 1870 near Duluth, and by 1873, the tracks from this iron-mining region reached St. Paul. Ten years later, the Northern Pacific completed its transcontinental line, following the route of the Lewis and Clark expedition to Puget Sound.

Interestingly enough, the Great Northern and the Northern Pa-

cific railways shared a headquarters building in downtown St. Paul. Although the competitors shared the building, the companies were sealed off from each other except for the employee cafeteria on the 13th floor.

While the Great Northern and the Northern Pacific were racing to connect Minnesota to the west, the Chicago, Burlington & Quincy Railroad was hurrying to complete its line from Chicago to St. Paul. Hill always dreamed of uniting his railroad with the Northern Pacific and the Chicago, Burlington & Quincy.

But it was not until 1970, nearly 55 years after his death, that Hill's vision was realized when the three railroads joined. Burlington Northern merged in 1980 with the St. Louis

& San Francisco Railway and in 1996 with the Atchison, Topeka & Santa Fe Railway to become BNSF.

Today, with 34,000 miles of track running throughout the United States and Canada, BNSF is one of the largest railroads in the world. The company's headquarters is in Fort Worth, but approximately 400 employees still report to duty at the site of the Great Northern and Northern Pacific headquarters building, now called the First Trust Center, in downtown St. Paul.

The mission of the BNSF railroad today is a different type of empire building than that of Hill's day. The railroad's motto—We Can Move Your World—describes its position as a premier transportation service provider. In 1999, BNSF hauled enough coal to generate nearly 10 percent of the nation's electricity, and is the largest transporter of grain, aluminum, aircraft parts, and beer by rail in the United States.

What began in St. Paul with a single locomotive and two cars traveling between St. Paul and Minneapolis continues today with 5,000 locomotives and 90,000 freight cars developing and supporting the nation's commerce. With its distinguished history and reputation, the Burlington Northern and Santa Fe Railway Company will be a transportation mainstay for generations to come.

WHAT BEGAN IN ST. PAUL WITH A SINGLE LOCOMOTIVE AND TWO CARS TRAVELING BETWEEN ST. PAUL AND MINNEAPOLIS CONTINUES TODAY WITH THE BURLINGTON NORTHERN AND SANTA FE RAILWAY COMPANY'S 5,000 LOCOMOTIVES AND 90,000 FREIGHT CARS DEVELOPING AND SUPPORTING THE NATION'S COMMERCE.

THE BNSF MOTTO—WE CAN MOVE YOUR WORLD—DESCRIBES ITS POSITION AS A PREMIER TRANSPORTATION SERVICE PROVIDER.

A T THE REQUEST OF BISHOP THOMAS GRACE, SIX SISTERS FROM THE Order of the Visitation made an uncertain steamboat voyage up the Mississippi River from St. Louis in 1873 to start a school in St. Paul. More than 125 years later, the values and ideals that those brave women brought with them live on at the institution they founded, Convent of the Visitation School.

Following the teachings of the founders, Saints Francis de Sales and Jane de Chantal, the 50-acre campus located just outside of St. Paul is permeated with a spirit of gentle strength, respect, courtesy, and healthy optimism. Cooperation is emphasized over competition at each of the age or grade levels—from the infants and toddlers in the child care center to the senior girls in the college preparatory high school program.

STRONG VALUES, STRONG ACADEMICS

Visitation School is an independent Catholic day school for boys and girls from Montessori preschool through grade six, and a college preparatory high school for young women in grades seven through 12—the only such high school in Minnesota. After sixth grade, many of the boys attend neighboring St. Thomas Academy, which is an all-boys school for grades seven through 12.

The tranquil Convent of the Visitation School campus is also home to a small group of sisters of the Visitation Order, a semicloistered, contemplative order that views relationships among people as key to a relationship with God. The sisters are no longer classroom teachers, but are role models who inspire students and faculty with their humble and gentle way of interacting with the school community.

"Seeing an eighth grader helping a first grader tie his shoe—that's a Visitation moment," says Patty Healy, director of admissions and marketing. With the convent just steps away from the classrooms, four generations are able to interact on campus.

DEVELOPING THE WHOLE STUDENT

The school imparts the teachings of the Catholic faith and encourages spiritual growth by urging students to live out their faith in ways that go beyond attending liturgy or religion class. Service to the community is important, and the entire school participates in food and clothing drives. Students in Campus Ministry visit nursing homes, work with physically and mentally challenged children, and provide layettes for the new babies of low-income families or single mothers.

Visitation strives to support and nurture each student's total development—spiritual, social, emotional, and academic. Small classes allow maximum participation and individual attention, which build knowledge and self-esteem. Visitation's SAT scores consistently surpass the national mean scores for females, and a remarkable 100 percent of the young women who graduate from Visitation's upper school go on to college.

The school's curriculum provides 16 advanced placement and honors courses, as well as a nationally recognized fine arts program. Performing arts opportunities for students include orchestra, choir, and theater productions. The new athletic center and fine arts facility demonstrate the school's commitment to athletics and the arts.

Convent of the Visitation School's commitment to developing the whole child—mind, body, and spirit—is summed up in its motto: Not for School, but for Life.

W HILE THE SAINT PAUL AREA CHAMBER OF COMMERCE HAS BEEN AT the heart of the area's business community for 132 years, it is by no means a stodgy, historic relic. With nearly 1,700 members, it is the largest local chamber in Minnesota and is a model of dynamic business advocacy for the future. "We're doing a lot that is innovative

for the chamber industry," says President Larry Dowell. "We're out front on issues of government and technology. We take a lead role and have become somewhat of a standard in the Upper Midwest."

One example of the creative approach the chamber has taken involves the recently built arena for St. Paul's new National Hockey League team, the Wild. Because so many of the chamber's members participated in helping to bring the team to St. Paul and to secure the construction of the arena, the chamber purchased a suite to serve its members. Now, any chamber member may lease this special suite to view Wild games.

"A small company can entertain clients or associates in style for an evening," Dowell says. "Buying the suite was a significant risk and something outside of the norm for chambers of commerce."

ST. PAUL'S BUSINESS ADVOCATE

W ith a commitment to excellence and a sense of fun, the chamber is constantly growing to better serve the business community. It currently draws 4,500

representatives from its 1,700 member companies—both large and small in St. Paul and the East Metro area—with its open and personable atmosphere and with its bold advocacy for businesses of all sizes. As Dowell says, "We are the unapologetic voice of business at the capitol."

With the state capitol just up the hill, this chamber has a unique proximity to the legislators who are setting the policies that will affect business. "We are the second home to every business across the state," says Dowell.

Taking a proactive approach to political affairs, the Saint Paul Area

Chamber of Commerce has a political action committee (PAC) to lobby state and local government officials on issues affecting business. The chamber works to elect qualified people to office, and makes a concerted effort to educate employers and employees about the political process and how they can have an impact.

"We're not afraid to have a PAC," Dowell notes, saying that the chamber doesn't shrink from taking a strong stand on local issues. For instance, the chamber lobbied in support of building a new baseball stadium in St. Paul. "It challenged

PROVIDING LEADERSHIP FOR THE SAINT PAUL AREA CHAMBER OF COMMERCE, PRESIDENT LARRY DOWELL DIRECTS THE VISION OF THE GROWING ENTITY.

WITH NEARLY 1,700 MEMBERS, THE SAINT PAUL AREA CHAMBER OF COMMERCE IS THE LARGEST LOCAL CHAMBER IN MINNESOTA AND A MODEL OF DYNAMIC BUSINESS ADVOCACY FOR THE FUTURE.

WITH A COMMITMENT TO EXCELLENCE AND A SENSE OF FUN, THE CHAMBER IS CONSTANTLY GROWING TO BETTER SERVE THE BUSINESS COMMUNITY.

residents to think about what they wanted their community to be," says Dowell. "We weren't in it for public opinion polls. We stuck it out and we're proud of that."

FOR THE PEOPLE

Beyond promoting economic growth and competitiveness on the larger governmental scale, the chamber is an important resource for individual businesses of all sizes. The network of members offers a vast wealth of knowledge and experience to the organization.

"We're not about things. We're about people, talents, and energy," Dowell says. "Our best resource is our human resource."

A dedicated team of volunteers helps drive the chamber's many initiatives. And this team represents a diverse cross section of the area's business community—from large corporations to a sole proprietor working out of his or her home.

Beyond offering opportunities for businesses to network with each other, the chamber connects employers with job seekers during this time of unprecedented labor shortages. Employer Solutions Inc., a nonprofit organization developed by and in partnership with the chamber, offers employers free job postings, a community-based Internet recruiting Web site, assessment, and referral, as well as educational and consulting services.

The Saint Paul Area Chamber of Commerce Foundation partners with area education projects, and

has provided grants and scholarships to help build a pool of qualified workers, ensuring that members have the necessary tools to recruit and retain high-caliber employees. The chamber encourages entrepreneurial spirit and innovative business ideas by offering small businesses advice, resources, and special programs such as MBA in a Day, designed to help a small business maintain its competitive edge.

"We want everyone to be able to realize the American dream," says Dowell. "Plus, you never know who will be the next 3M."

GROUNDWORK FOR THE FUTURE

While the Saint Paul Area Chamber of Commerce's roots in St. Paul run deep, the chamber's vision is far reaching. Chamber leadership understands the opportunities and challenges the

global economy and fast-moving technology present to business people today. "We're very attuned to the global marketplace and technology, and how to use it to make sound business decisions," Dowell says.

The chamber recently entered into a sister city relationship with Neuss, Germany. Rather than the traditional cultural exchange, the chamber sees the partnership as an opportunity for economic development on both sides of the Atlantic. Trade missions, as well as one-on-one business exchanges in St. Paul and Nuess, are planned.

With its vigorous growth in membership, innovative initiatives, and global perspective, the Saint Paul Area Chamber of Commerce is poised to be a vibrant force for the St. Paul and East Metro-area business community for the next century and beyond.

M. R. DANIELSON ADVERTISING

BEYOND PROMOTING ECONOMIC GROWTH AND COMPETITIVENESS ON THE LARGER GOVERNMENTAL SCALE, THE SAINT PAUL AREA CHAMBER OF COMMERCE IS AN IMPORTANT RESOURCE FOR INDIVIDUAL BUSINESSES OF ALL SIZES.

REGIONS HOSPITAL, A PRIVATE, FULL-SERVICE MEDICAL CENTER, HAS BEEN an integral part of the St. Paul community for more than 128 years. Today, with new facilities, state-of-the-art technology, and an innovative philosophy of care, Regions Hospital is addressing the health care needs of the region for the next century. ▨ "We are building on

our foundation of innovative programs, including our widely recognized burn center, Level I trauma center, and emergency center," says Terry S. Finzen, president and CEO of Regions Hospital. "We're also looked upon for our programs of excellence in critical care, heart disease, seniors, women's services, cancer, and other specialty areas. We will continue to add programs and services to support our vision of being the patient-centered hospital of choice for our community."

Region Hospital's recent, $62.5 million building expansion and renovation project was the largest single expansion and renovation in the hospital's history. Expansion 2000 is the result of a long-term, comprehensive strategic planning process to enable the hospital to meet the care needs of patients for the coming decades. The project added 230,000 square feet of new and remodeled space to Regions Hospital.

A HEALING ENVIRONMENT

Regions Hospital's new and renovated facilities were designed to create a healing environment through a thoughtful blend of physical design, medical

technology, and the nursing staff's holistic approach to patient care.

"We are transforming Regions Hospital into an environment that is conducive to healing—one that recognizes the need to heal not only the body, but the mind and spirit as well," says Bill Knutson, senior vice president and COO at Regions Hospital.

Components of the healing environment include subtle design elements that reduce stress, such as a muted color scheme, minimized noise, artwork reminiscent of nature, a three-story atrium with

windows that overlook a landscaped garden, and privacy throughout.

Regions Hospital is one of the first hospitals in the Twin Cities to incorporate a holistic approach to nursing. In selected areas, patients have the opportunity to choose therapies such as massage, breathing and relaxation techniques, music, meditation, aromatherapy, and even pet visits. Nursing staff also have been trained to work with patients to examine how physical, emotional, and spiritual aspects of their lives may contribute to their illness, and help them form healthy new habits.

"Holistic nursing just simply gets to the core of what we are about as professionals," says Diane McEllistrem, RN, a certified holistic nurse. "We're here to offer as much support, education, and guidance as the patient chooses to accept."

DEPTH OF RESOURCES

An important part of the healing environment is the peace of mind patients have when they know that all the health care resources they may need are close at hand, including an expert medical staff and a full range of specialists.

At Regions Hospital Heart Center, for instance, a full array of cardiovascular services is available,

THE GUEST SERVICES STAFF AT REGIONS HOSPITAL ASSISTS VISITORS WITH INFORMATION ABOUT HOSPITAL AND NEIGHBORHOOD SERVICES.

THE EMERGENCY CENTER AT REGIONS HOSPITAL IS EQUIPPED TO CARE FOR PATIENTS WITH A BROAD RANGE OF ILLNESSES AND INJURIES.

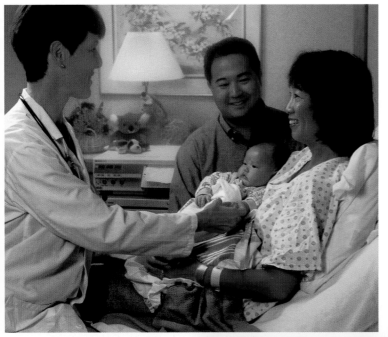

from diagnostic tests to surgery to rehabilitation programs and educational resources. A skilled team of cardiologists and cardiothoracic surgeons staff the center. The echocardiography laboratory at Regions Hospital Heart Center is the first in the metropolitan area to achieve full accreditation for its quality of care in three treatment methods by the American College of Cardiology and the American Society of Echocardiography. This prestigious accreditation was earned in transthoracic, stress, and transesophageal treatment.

The hospital's Cancer Care Program is also recognized as an American College of Surgeons-accredited teaching hospital. The Regions Hospital PartneringCare® Senior Services has been recognized nationally by *U.S. News & World Report* for its quality, comprehensive care programs for seniors.

The birth center offers services for mother, baby, and the entire family. Physicians, certified nurse midwives, and lactation consultants are on staff, and a neonatal intensive care unit is available if necessary. The newly built center includes private rooms with garden views and space for partners to stay overnight during this special time.

With the only Level I trauma center in the east metropolitan area, Regions Hospital is standing by with surgeons and other critical care specialists, ready to care for the most severely injured adults and children. At the same time,

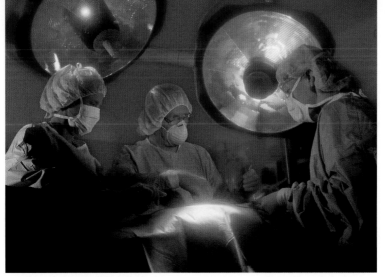

the hospital's emergency center provides the highest level of service to patients with a variety of illnesses and injuries.

Regions Hospital is world renowned for its burn center, one of the country's first, founded in 1963. Here, all services have been consolidated in one area, from the outpatient clinic to the intensive care units and rehabilitation rooms. The center also includes sleeping rooms and a rooftop garden for families.

COMMUNITY SERVICE

Regions Hospital, which is part of the HealthPartners family of health care organizations, serves the community in less obvious ways as well. As a teaching and research institution, the hospital is intimately involved in training the next generation of physicians, and

is on the cutting edge of medical technology and research to improve care.

In an even more tangible way, Regions Hospital serves the surrounding community with its health resource center, which is open to the public and offers books, magazines, videos, and computers with Internet access to information about a wide variety of health issues. Regions Hospital is also committed to meeting the health care needs of low-income area residents, and continues to serve the uninsured members of the community.

"We are proud of the services and programs that we provide our community," says Finzen. Regions Hospital is committed to continuing the tradition of quality established when it began serving the area in 1872.

WEST GROUP, LOCATED IN THE ST. PAUL SUBURB OF EAGAN, IS A leading provider of e-information and solutions to the U.S. legal market. First established in 1872 as John B. West, Publisher and Bookseller, this St. Paul company grew quickly into a well-known and highly respected name in the legal information industry.

For more than 125 years, West Group has excelled in the legal information industry and has been at the leading edge of innovation at every point along the way.

POSITIONED FOR THE FUTURE

West Group may be more than a century old, but the company breaks the mold of the traditional law book publisher. In addition to providing products in print and on CD-ROM, West Group is also a leading provider of Web-based services for the legal community. With a focus on technology and the ability to deliver its products and services through cutting-edge channels, West Group remains a leader in today's information technology revolution. The company houses one of the largest data centers in the Midwest.

West Group uses its technological resources and expertise to provide revolutionary tools for lawyers. For example, its Westlaw® on-line research tool was launched to the legal community in 1975, and today contains more than 14,000 legal, regulatory, and business information databases. KeyCite®, West Group's citation research service,

helps lawyers tell whether a case or statute is still "good law," and provides lawyers with vital, up-to-the-minute coverage of legal developments. And *Law*office.com™, one of West Group's most recently introduced on-line services, helps consumers and small-business owners understand their legal needs and find professional help. Other West Group solutions include WestWorks™, the legal industry's first integrated practice management and research suite, and WestFile®, an electronic court filing service.

"We believe that content, coupled with superior technology, provides a new level of power and functionality to our customers," explains Michael E. Wilens, president. "The Web is one of our key conduits for delivering information and solutions to legal professionals. It's also the focus for how we develop products and do business—with a strong e-mind-set and customer focus that lets us create better products more quickly."

With its strong history, unparalleled name recognition, and extensive resources, West Group is focused on the future. By capitalizing on emerging innovations and continually developing technologies, the company stays ahead of the curve of change in today's evolving marketplace. In response to this changing environment, West Group has focused on developing an e-business culture where its employees are offered unlimited opportunities for growth.

AN EMPLOYER OF CHOICE

West Group—which considers itself to be about people—is committed to attracting, retaining, and developing the best and brightest personnel. As an employer of choice, West Group provides its some 7,500 employees with a

FIRST ESTABLISHED IN 1872 AS JOHN B. WEST, PUBLISHER AND BOOKSELLER, WEST GROUP HAS BECOME A HIGHLY RESPECTED NAME IN THE LEGAL INFORMATION INDUSTRY BY USING TECHNOLOGICAL RESOURCES AND EXPERTISE TO PROVIDE REVOLUTIONARY TOOLS FOR LAWYERS.

progressive work environment that encourages innovation and development opportunities. The company's unique emphasis on the individual has been highlighted by both the national and local media, and has been recognized by several outside organizations.

West Group's accolades include being named one of the 100 Best Companies for Working Mothers by *Working Mother* magazine in 1999 and 2000, and the Best of the Best by the Master Printers of America in its 2000 Best Workplace in America competition. West Group also received Minnesota Women Lawyers' 2000 Leadership Award, awarded each year to a legal employer that has demonstrated leadership in the employment of women in the workplace.

In line with the firm's commitment to its staff, West Group has established many programs that help employees balance their work and personal life. For example, West Group provides flexible work arrangements, a telecommuting pilot program, dependent care programs, and a tuition reimbursement program for employees interested in obtaining an undergraduate, graduate, or postgraduate degree at an accredited educational institution.

Thomson University, West Group's center for personal and professional development, helps facilitate knowledge sharing and an e-business culture. The university's on-site learning center provides classes in such areas as career guidance and management, as well as performance consulting services. Thomson University also offers self-paced learning programs; team building; technology- and

Internet-based programs; and library and information search services and videoconferencing. West Group places a strong emphasis on implementing programs that contribute not only to the success of the business, but also to the growth and development of employees in all facets of their lives.

"We realize that our employees are key to our success, which is why we strive to recognize each person's individual contributions to our business," says Wilens. "By providing numerous training opportunities, along with a range of services and amenities, we help people enhance their professional and personal development. We also believe that this environment creates numerous knowledge sharing

opportunities, which in turn provide West Group with a competitive advantage."

West Group is part of The Thomson Corporation, a leading global e-information and solutions company serving the business and professional marketplace. West Group's campus in Eagan also serves as the headquarters for Thomson Legal & Regulatory, the largest market group within The Thomson Corporation. Together with other Thomson Legal & Regulatory businesses around the globe, West Group serves legal professionals in more than 23 countries. From Eagan to New York to London to Sydney, West Group is poised to continue leading the way for centuries to come.

IN LINE WITH THE COMPANY'S COMMITMENT TO ITS PEOPLE, WEST GROUP HAS ESTABLISHED MANY PROGRAMS THAT HELP EMPLOYEES BALANCE THEIR WORK AND PERSONAL LIVES.

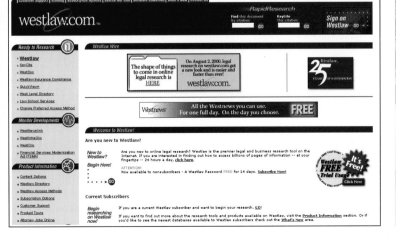

FOR MORE THAN 125 YEARS, WEST GROUP HAS EXCELLED IN THE LEGAL INFORMATION INDUSTRY AND HAS BEEN AT THE LEADING EDGE OF INNOVATION AT EVERY POINT ALONG THE WAY.

AT&T

THERE'S A WORLD OF AT&T IN MINNESOTA. THOUSANDS OF AT&T employees, including hundreds in St. Paul, call Minnesota home. These employees supply residential customers with broadband digital video, local phone, and Internet services. And they pair customers with the right wireless services to fit their individual needs.

AT&T employees in Minnesota set up national and international teleconference calls. They respond to customer service inquiries over the phone and on the Internet. And they build and maintain the highly advanced digital telecommunications network that connects Minnesota to the rest of the world.

With landmark buildings in both downtowns—along the Mississippi River in St. Paul and on the Skyway System in the heart of downtown Minneapolis—AT&T is omnipresent in Minnesota.

But that's not all. AT&T's commitment to community includes a strong history of corporate volunteerism and philanthropy. AT&T services, grants, and employees are at work in neighborhood schools and with local nonprofit organizations.

AN ESTABLISHED LEADER

In 1879, AT&T became the first company to bring telephone service to Minnesota. Also, in the latter half of the 19th century, the company appropriated the Bell System, which, at the time, was the undisputed world leader in telephone service. As a result of a 1984 agreement between AT&T and the U.S. Department of Justice, the corporation was divided into eight companies; from 1984 until 1996, AT&T succeeded in the new, more open market as an integrated telecommunications services and equipment company.

Now, as AT&T expands its horizons to include voice, data, and video services, the company is once again the industry leader, outstripping its competitors in providing long-distance and business service plans. AT&T continues to introduce technological firsts to residents and businesses in Minnesota as it builds and operates the world's most sophisticated wire and wireless networks.

AT&T BROADBAND

Since the summer of 2000, St. Paul area cable television customers have been served by AT&T Broadband, which completed its merger with MediaOne in June 2000. But AT&T Broadband means more than cable television to St. Paul.

By investing more than $250 million to upgrade AT&T's existing coaxial cable network with fiber-optic technology, AT&T is bringing the broadband revolution to the St. Paul area. The upgrade provides AT&T Broadband the necessary power and bandwidth to turn a former cable TV-only system into a telecommunications powerhouse that provides interactive digital cable TV, high-speed cable Internet service, and local digital telephone service. Soon, AT&T customers will be able to fulfill all their telecommunications requirements—voice, data, and video—through one company.

"There is a whole new world of choices in telecommunications," said Jim Commers, vice president of AT&T Broadband. "We now have the ability to have one company like AT&T deliver all of the customer's communications needs in one bundle. We're working to make that vision a reality."

While this upgrade and introduction of new products has increased customer choice, it also means that the company has become an even larger employer in St. Paul. But employment is not the only contribution AT&T Broadband makes in St. Paul.

In partnership with the cable industry, AT&T Broadband is an active supporter of Cable in the Classroom, which provides free cable TV service and programming to local schools. AT&T is also working hard to provide schools with free access to its high-speed Internet

In 1879, AT&T became the first company to bring telephone service to Minnesota.

service to help turn the classroom into a virtual learning center.

AT&T's mission of being a global broadband services provider will allow the company to provide a business' or an individual's telephone, wireless phone, cable television, and Internet hook-ups through a seamless network of technological systems. AT&T is a one-stop shop in the world of communication.

AT&T Wireless

In 1998, AT&T revolutionized the wireless communications industry by introducing the digital one-rate plan, which carries no extra charge for roaming or long-distance calls.

"We were the first wireless company to step up to the plate and say, 'This is the right thing to do,' " says Steve Elm, vice president and general manager of AT&T Wireless. "It really forced other carriers to do the same thing to compete, and led to the surge in mergers across the country."

AT&T Wireless prides itself on being at the forefront of this fast-moving industry, with a record of innovative rate plans and products for its customers. With stores throughout the Twin Cities metro area, AT&T Wireless and its approximately 1,000 local employees are able to meet business and residential customers' diverse needs. In addition, two of the company's major call centers, servicing customers across the country, are located in the region.

AT&T plans to be instrumental in the next generation of wireless products, including Edge technology—the coming upgrade from digi-

tal technology—and enhanced 911, which will allow emergency dispatchers to pinpoint the location of people calling from cell phones. Wireless data products, such as Internet access, are an important component of the full line of products and services AT&T Wireless is continually refining in order to keep providing customers with the best and latest technology.

While AT&T Wireless offers a world of service to its customers, it also serves the St. Paul community. AT&T Wireless is a longtime sponsor of the St. Paul Saints baseball team, as well as a member

of the Capitol Cities Partnership. AT&T's All-American Digital Dog Snoopy was a favorite in the Peanuts on Parade, and was auctioned off for $25,000 to benefit the Charles Schulz Memorial Fund.

The company also works as a partner with the St. Paul Area Red Cross in assembling the winter driving safety kits offered each year. Finally, AT&T Wireless is one of the founding members of the Minnesota Wireless Foundation, which was formed to promote safe and responsible use of cell phones—another instance of the company's civic commitment.

AT&T's All-American Digital Dog Snoopy was a favorite in the Peanuts on Parade, and was auctioned off for $25,000 to benefit the Charles Schulz Memorial Fund.

NE OF AMERICA'S MOST HIGHLY RATED FINANCIAL INSTITUTIONS, MINNESOTA Life provides financial security for individuals and businesses in the form of insurance, pensions, and investments. ⊠ Founded in 1880, Minnesota Life has established a successful tradition of steady growth, based on quality products, fundamental values, and sound

investment strategies. Today, more than 4,400 home office associates and field representatives—located at the company's St. Paul head-quarters and throughout the country—design, sell, and service a broad range of financial products.

Minnesota Life continuously adapts to the world around it to protect the company's financial strength and to ensure its ability to serve both current and future clients. Technology, which includes on-line services such

as the company's Web site at www.minnesotalife.com, plays an increasingly important role in the products and services provided in all of the company's business areas.

SERVING SPECIFIC MARKETS

Each of the company's five strategic business units has a defined purpose and specific target markets, yet all five share a common goal: to be the best at providing

financial security and value for clients.

Minnesota Life's career agency system is the cornerstone of its Individual Insurance business unit, providing the link with individual clients-affluent business owners, professionals, and executives. The company offers a diversified portfolio of risk protection and wealth accumulation products, including adjustable life insurance, which it pioneered in 1971, and a wide range of variable life insurance products.

The company's Financial Services business unit works with thousands of banks and credit unions to provide mortgage disability and home owners protection for the firm's clients. Minnesota Life dominates the mortgage life market as its leading writer, and is the second-leading insurer in the credit union market. With the only nationwide career sales force exclusively serving the mortgage market, the company's marketing strength is amplified through electronic links with various financial institutions.

The Group Insurance business unit serves large, well-known employers who have complex employee benefit and tax-planning requirements. Minnesota Life is the only insurer endorsed by farm credit associations in all 50 states, and maintains a solid 90 percent market share of the life insurance sold through the farm credit system. In addition to large employers and agricultural groups, the company provides extensive coverage to professional associations across the United States.

Minnesota Life's Retirement Plan Services division provides employers with enduring retirement plan solutions for participants' retirement security. The company offers both full-service and un-bundled approaches to 401(k), defined benefit, money purchase, and profit sharing plans. Minnesota

MINNESOTA LIFE HAS CALLED ST. PAUL HOME SINCE THE COMPANY'S FOUNDING IN 1880.

Life provides its plan sponsors with sound plan design, flexible data management, coordinated and timely plan implementation, seamless administration, self-service employee communication, and educational tools that build participation and help employees reach their financial goals.

Minnesota Life's investment subsidiary, Advantus Capital Management, Inc., manages the company's assets. In addition, Advantus serves as an investment adviser primarily to smaller insurance companies with between $50 million and $5 billion of assets. Seeking performance advantage with minimum risk potential, Advantus' investment professionals provide the sophisticated asset management needed to cope with today's complex and dynamic investment environment.

FINDING AND KEEPING THE BEST

Minnesota Life gives the highest priority to the needs of its employees. Opportunities for growth are part of the company's commitment to every employee. Minnesota Life is particularly proud of its associate retention levels.

"This is a good place to make a home," says Robert L. Senkler, chairman and CEO. "It is a good place to grow in your career and do something worthwhile."

The company's commitment to community involvement and a family-friendly workplace has earned it national recognition for corporate citizenship from the White House. *Computerworld* magazine recently rated Minnesota Life as one of the 100 best places to work in the country for the fifth year in a row.

The company believes it is simply good business to provide associates the tools necessary to become the very best at what they do. Minnesota Life provides exceptional internal training and encourages associates to take advantage of tuition reimbursement for college courses. The firm's benefit package ranks in the upper tier for companies of its size, and Minnesota Life fosters a balanced approach to work and home life, recognizing that maintaining a sharp focus at work

necessitates a commitment to life outside the office.

Over the years, Minnesota Life's pioneering products, service commitment, and conservative invest-

ment philosophy, as well as the exceptionally high quality of its workforce, have combined to make the company a national leader in financial services.

MINNESOTA LIFE HAS ESTABLISHED A SUCCESSFUL TRADITION OF STEADY GROWTH, BASED ON QUALITY PRODUCTS, FUNDAMENTAL VALUES, AND SOUND INVESTMENT STRATEGIES (TOP).

A MINNESOTA LIFE EMPLOYEE FOR MORE THAN 25 YEARS, CHAIRMAN AND CEO ROBERT L. SENKLER HELPS MAINTAIN THE COMPANY'S TRADITION OF TRUST, STRENGTH, AND INTEGRITY. "WE SELL A PROMISE TO PAY, AND OUR STRONG FINANCIAL POSITION UNDERSCORES OUR ABILITY TO FULFILL ALL OF OUR OBLIGATIONS," SAYS SENKLER. "WE WILL BE THERE WHEN OUR CLIENTS NEED US" (BOTTOM).

WELLS FARGO & COMPANY

I**T'S A WINTER DAY IN THE BEGINNING OF THE 20TH CENTURY IN ST. PAUL.** Despite the cold, the photographer insists on taking the employee photograph outside, choosing as his prop one of several Wells Fargo & Co. Express sleds that roam the snow-packed city, delivering packages at all hours. ▨ Men pause in their work and gather on the sled, their

worn coats unbuttoned to shed the heat of labor. Two derby-wearing managers tromp from their office and perch on the sled's back. A flash of magnesium powder, a click, and it's done. The men clamber down and nonchalantly get back to business, but the photograph can't disguise the look of pride—and, in the case of the jaunty young man in the middle, the joy—they take in their work.

This was Wells Fargo in 1900, a combination bank and delivery service with 10,000 locations across the United States. Welcome to the new Wells Fargo, a company that is no stranger to St. Paul. The new Wells Fargo is the nation's most

admired bank, according to a recent edition of *Fortune* magazine. It's a product of the merger between Norwest Corporation and the old Wells Fargo & Company, which survived the government takeover of its national delivery franchise in 1918 and, decades later, emerged as one of the nation's leading financial services companies. By combining the best of both companies, the new Wells Fargo offers customers the widest range of financial services products found anywhere.

Wells Fargo & Company has 15,500 team members in Minnesota, and is a national leader in small-business lending, agricultural lending, on-line financial services, mortgage originations, education financing, commercial real estate lending, and insurance industry sales. The firm's vision is to become the premier financial services company in North America, satisfying all of the financial needs of its customers and helping them succeed financially.

At Wells Fargo, it all starts with people: team members, customers, and communities. Team members are the firm's most important competitive advantage. Believing that people choose to do business with other people, not a company, Wells Fargo works to become the company of choice by attracting, developing, retaining, and motivating a

diverse team of talented people. The firm considers the attitude of its team members to be the most important difference between a good financial services company and a great one.

For instance, Wells Fargo is the state's largest contributor of instructors to Junior Achievement, helping schools teach financial management skills to students of all ages. St. Paul team members contributed time and talent in 1994 to one of the company's first Habitat for Humanity work projects on the city's East Side. Team members have taken part in other Habitat projects in St. Paul, and have joined in the annual Paint-A-Thon and Brush with Kindness home beautification programs.

"A company with employees who care about their work, coupled with decentralized decision making, is an unbeatable combination," says Joan Grzywinski, president of Wells Fargo & Company in St. Paul. "Our predecessor bank in St. Paul was Empire National Bank, which joined the old Northwest Bancorporation in the year of its founding, 1929. Since then, we've grown through outstanding customer service and acquisitions. Today, we're one of the major banks in St. Paul and we look forward to continuing to contribute to our city's success."

TO TRANSPORT GOODS BETWEEN THE RAIL DEPOT AND THE ST. PAUL OFFICE ONE BLOCK AWAY, WELLS FARGO CALLED ON THE SERVICES OF A WORKHORSE NAMED BILLY, WHOSE STRENGTH AT PULLING A TRAIN OF LOADED CARTS EARNED HIM THE MONIKER WELLS FARGO & COMPANY'S SWITCH ENGINE (TOP).

WELLS FARGO HAS MORE THAN 3,000 BANKING STORES ACROSS THE NATION STAFFED WITH FINANCIAL SERVICE EXPERTS WHO ARE READY TO HELP (BOTTOM LEFT AND RIGHT).

MINNESOTA HISTORICAL SOCIETY

MARTIN PHOTOMEDIA

MARTIN PHOTOMEDIA

TOLTZ, KING, DUVALL, ANDERSON & ASSOCIATES, INC. (TKDA) has helped shape St. Paul and the surrounding region in a very substantial way. Many of the landmarks that distinguish the city were designed and engineered by this firm of engineers, architects, and planners, which celebrated its 90th year of excellence in 2000.

"We are unique because of our longevity and the fact that we've spent all of our 90 years in St. Paul," says Darrel H. Berkowitz, president and CEO of TKDA. "We have a reputation of serving clients over four or five generations. The way we operate decade after decade means they can trust TKDA generation after generation."

TKDA's portfolio of clients reads like a checklist of major local corporations: 3M; Andersen Corporation; Burlington Northern & Santa Fe Railway; Cargill, Inc.; Alliant Techsystems, Inc.; and the City of St. Paul itself.

GROWTH AND PROSPERITY

In fact, the growth of TKDA over the last century mirrors that of the city. Max Toltz, the founder of the firm, was a German-born structural engineer who became the chief bridge engineer on the Great Northern Railway, working under James J. Hill, the industrialist who helped put St. Paul on the map.

In 1910, Toltz left Hill's railway to start the Toltz Engineering Company, locating his business in the heart of downtown St. Paul. One of the firm's early projects was the structural engineering for St. Paul Cathedral, which was dedicated in 1915. The cathedral's green dome was modeled on St. Peter's in Rome, and still awes visitors and serves as a striking landmark visible from many points in downtown. The firm's projects in St. Paul include designing the Robert Street Bridge, Como Park Conservatory, and Hamm Building, among others.

Toltz's company flourished and, in 1956, changed its name to Toltz, King, Duvall, Anderson & Associates, Inc. to reflect its growing partnerships. As a tribute to its founder on TKDA's 90th anniversary, a cutout statue of Toltz circulated throughout each department so employees could learn about and remember the man who started the company nearly a century ago.

TODAY'S TKDA

Today, TKDA is made up of three comprehensive divisions—transportation, building design, and municipal/environmental—bringing 200 employees representing more than 16 professional disciplines to downtown St. Paul each day.

Each division continues to leave its mark on the city in both the private and the public sector. Recent projects have included many of the state-of-the-art educational and sports buildings at local colleges and universities, the taxiways and a runway at Minneapolis/St. Paul International Airport, the Canadian Pacific Railway Yard fueling facility, and rehabilitation of some of the city's landmarks. For instance, TKDA was instrumental in rebuilding the historic Wabasha Street Bridge, which connects the east and west sides of the city.

The company also leaves its mark in less tangible ways through its community involvement. Working with the Boy Scouts, TKDA has organized a program to introduce high school and college students to the fields of engineering, architecture, and planning by offering internships. TKDA employees have mentored St. Paul fifth and sixth graders in math, and purchased special mathematics computer programs for their school. The American Cancer Society recently recognized TKDA for being an outstanding company in support of cancer patients.

"We're very active in the community," Berkowitz says. "And we've got a great story to tell."

TKDA PROVIDED ARCHITECTURAL AND ENGINEERING SERVICES FOR THE HAMM BUILDING IN DOWNTOWN ST. PAUL (LEFT).

IN 1915, TOLTZ, KING, DUVALL, ANDERSON & ASSOCIATES, INC. PROVIDED STRUCTURAL ENGINEERING SERVICES FOR ST. PAUL CATHEDRAL (RIGHT).

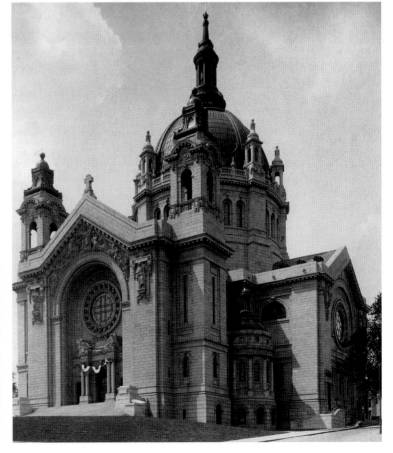

OST PEOPLE PROBABLY ARE NOT AWARE OF THE IMPACT MINNESOTA Mining and Manufacturing (3M) has on their daily lives. But look around and the St. Paul company's first century of innovative products is evident just about everywhere—from the sponge beside the sink, to the Scotch® Transparent Tape on gifts, to the omnipresent Post-it® Notes.

The diversified manufacturing company's innovations also touch people in less visible ways as well, with health care products that help prevent infection, protect skin, and dispense medication; reflective sheeting products that make road signs brighter and easier to see; and electronic devices and sophisticated optical systems that allow businesses to work smarter.

Today, on the verge of its second century, 3M employs more than 70,000 people, and manufactures more than 50,000 products for the industrial, commercial, consumer, and health care markets. In 1999, the company's sales totaled $15.7 billion.

HARD-EARNED SUCCESS

It all started in 1902, when five businessmen in northern Minnesota founded 3M to mine what they thought was corundum, a mineral ideal for making sandpaper and grinding wheels. The mineral they found, however, was a poor quality anorthosite. There was only one sale of the abrasive and the company almost failed.

But the founders were determined to succeed, so they shifted the focus to sandpaper production, purchasing abrasive minerals from another source. In 1910, with the support of St. Paul businessman Lucius Ordway and the vision of hardworking sales manager William L. McKnight, 3M moved production to St. Paul.

In 1916, the company established its first research and development laboratory. 3M also paid its first dividend of six cents a share, and has never missed a payment to its shareholders since. The company's president at the time, Edgar Ober, said, "There are a lot of people who thought we'd never make it." But just a year later, in 1917, 3M sales reached $1 million—and it has continued to grow ever since.

Innovation has been the

THE 3M GENERAL LABORATORY, IN WHICH THE COMPANY'S FIRST FORMAL PRODUCT RESEARCH BEGAN, ESTABLISHED SCIENTIFIC QUALITY CONTROL STANDARDS FOR COATED ABRASIVES.

3M CENTER—3M'S WORLD HEADQUARTERS IN ST. PAUL—IS THE HUB OF THE COMPANY'S GLOBAL RESEARCH NETWORK AND THE WORK SITE OF MORE THAN 11,500 EMPLOYEES.

company's passion since its earliest days. The focus is on identifying and anticipating needs in a variety of industries and addressing them creatively. Three-M-ite™ Abrasive Cloth was the company's first truly innovative product, and became a best-seller with the booming automobile industry and repair shops of the day. In the 1920s, 3M introduced its second revolutionary new product, Wetordry™ Waterproof Sandpaper. This product had applications not only in the car manufacturing business, but also in the kitchen to clean pots and pans. Thus, 3M diversified into the home market—setting the stage for a century of innovative products in new markets and accelerating growth.

By the end of the 1920s, 3M had become one of the first U.S. companies with the vision to look to overseas markets. Today, the company has operations in more than 60 countries.

In 1925, a young researcher named Richard Drew was striving to help automotive body painters maintain a clean edge on the popular two-tone-colored cars of the day. His quest led him to invent Scotch® Masking Tape to address this need. A few years later, Scotch® Cellophane Tape was born. Today, 3M manufactures more than 900 kinds of tape for multiple uses. On a larger scale, these first tapes mark the beginning of 3M's innovations in adhesives. Today's adhesives are on products that make it possible for consumers to hang pictures, decorations, or other objects without using nails.

During the Great Depression, the thrifty public found hundreds of ways to use Scotch cellophane tape and 3M prospered. Not a single 3M employee had to be let go during this time of economic turmoil.

PART OF THE COMMUNITY

With its roots firmly planted in St. Paul, 3M is known as a good corporate citizen here and around the world. The 3M Foundation was formed in 1953 as the charitable arm of the company, and invests in programs that support community needs in education, social, and economic development. In

1999, the 3M Foundation invested nearly $30 million in education and community life through financial and 3M product contributions.

"In our holistic approach, we are continually expanding our collaboration through community partnerships to meet the needs of the whole person," says David W. Powell, president of the 3M Foundation. "Our mission endures to support and inspire innovation that will strengthen education and life in 3M communities."

Examples of 3M's community involvement abound. Whether it is involvement in Junior Achievement, a neighborhood paint-a-thon project, or the coaching of young mathematicians, 3M employees volunteer many hours each year in their communities, while the foundation provides financial or product support. One of the projects supported by the foundation over the years has been subsidizing ticket prices for students to attend the performing arts classroom at the Ordway Center for the Performing Arts in downtown St. Paul.

Just as, nearly a century ago, Lucius Ordway stepped forward to help a struggling sandpaper company grow and prosper, now that same company, in turn, is helping to support the theater that bears the Ordway family name. For so many years and in so many ways, innovation and corporate citizenship have become hallmarks of 3M.

SCOTCH® POP-UP TAPE STRIPS, 3M'S LATEST TAPE REFINEMENT, FEATURE A DISPENSING SYSTEM THAT POPS UP PRECUT STRIPS OF TAPE TO MAKE TAPING JOBS EASIER.

3M EMPLOYS MORE THAN 70,000 PEOPLE AND MANUFACTURES MORE THAN 50,000 PRODUCTS FOR THE INDUSTRIAL, COMMERCIAL, CONSUMER, AND HEALTH CARE MARKETS.

A
NYONE WHO HAS EVER EATEN IN A RESTAURANT HAS PROBABLY SEEN National Checking Company's biggest selling product—the little green Guest Check pad that the wait staff uses to take orders. This simple, yet familiar item has helped earn National Checking Company a secure berth among the top 250 printing companies in the United States.

The success story of the company, however, goes beyond the popularity of the patented Guest Check. It really is a story of a small, privately owned business that has been able to evolve and adapt to a changing marketplace through some nine decades.

A CENTURY OF INNOVATION

I
n 1905, Carl Raschick founded the company "to engage in business as printers—to manufacture, buy, sell, import, export, and generally deal in cash registers, check, slip, and automatic printing registers." Raschick was a man

of great vision and foresaw the growth of the restaurant business. He thus positioned National Checking Company to fulfill the printing needs of that industry.

Printing the then-popular coupon books for schools, cafés, gas stations, and railroads was the company's primary focus in its early years. These coupons, rather than cash, were used in exchange for goods or services. For instance, some railroad employees were paid in food coupons rather than cash to reduce the odds that they would spend their pay on liquor and fail to report to work the next day.

Early on, National Checking Company held the patent on the Quicksend Check, a precursor to the Guest Check. A waitress would tally the price of a restaurant guest's meal on the Quicksend Check, and then tear the figure off the check for the customer to take to the register. Later, the company produced punch checks in which prices were preprinted on each page. The waitress would simply hand punch the appropriate price for the items ordered.

When the Guest Check made its debut in the 1920s, restaurants used the little pads for advertising by having them imprinted with the name of the establishment, a slogan, or a reminder on each sheet. A national sales team would sell these booklets directly to restaurateurs.

During World War II, material shortages made production of the firm's products difficult, but after the war, National Checking Company hit its stride again. The firm expanded its product line to include the cutting-edge technology of the day—the tab card. These data processing cards were used in early computers and were in great demand from companies such as 3M, Burlington Northern Railroad, Univac, and even NASA. By 1979, computers began using magnetic tape and microchips, prompting

the company to focus once more on its ever popular Guest Check in its various forms.

To increase efficiency and sales, National Checking Company shifted its marketing focus from individual restaurants to national distributors. In the 1970s, the firm began to distribute products through companies that supply restaurants with a full line of products in the serving of food. The strategy proved to be a great success.

"That marketing strategy was successful because we were always there with our product and sales support," says Rick Nelson, director of marketing at National Checking Company. "To help our distributors, we hold sales meetings, promotions, mailings, and anything necessary to get our product in front of the restaurateur. Our ability and willingness to work with the distributor have allowed us to establish our product niche."

An Order for Success

National Checking Company, which currently employs some 160 people, is headquartered on the Mississippi River in St. Paul. There, three shifts each day print, bind, and cut the various styles of Guest Checks and manufacture cash register rolls. Special machinery makes the job quieter and more efficient than the original deafening presses and labor-intensive methods used at the turn of the century.

"We're very much a family business—not only in the ownership ranks, but out on the floor," says Mark Hottinger, treasurer, referring to several longtime employees who work to bind the Guest Check pads or who direct the production process.

While the feeling is of a small, closely held business, National Checking Company has kept up with the competitive food service market by staying on top of technological advances. For instance, to accommodate the latest computer cash registers used by restaurants, the company now produces cash register, printer, and credit card rolls of paper. Additionally, each carton of products shipped includes a bar code on each side so that when a pallet of boxes arrives at a fully automated distribution warehouse, the code may be scanned and the products efficiently stored and shipped.

E-commerce through the company's Web site allows products sold through the distributor to be shipped directly from headquarters in St. Paul. "We've stayed on the cutting edge of technology to allow easy handling of our product," Nelson says. "We've also enlarged our business in the past two decades by buying two other companies." National Checking Company now owns Focus Business Graphics, a general business printer, and Midwest Business Forms, which produces business forms, as well as the multipart forms used to make certain Guest Checks.

Company President Ben Olk Jr. began working for the firm as a teenager, delivering checks to his father's Chicago accounts. "When we step back and look at how the company has moved technologically after 95 years of business," he says, "we realize how very dynamic and how much of a leader National Checking Company is in the area that we service."

THE STORY OF NATIONAL CHECKING COMPANY IS THE STORY OF A SMALL, PRIVATELY OWNED BUSINESS THAT HAS BEEN ABLE TO EVOLVE AND ADAPT TO THE CHANGING MARKETPLACE THROUGH SOME NINE DECADES.

THE ST. PAUL-AREA LANDSCAPE IS DOTTED WITH STRUCTURES DESIGNED and built by Ellerbe Becket since its founding in 1909 by Franklin Ellerbe. Since then, Ellerbe Becket has been bringing cutting-edge, innovative architectural design, engineering, and construction to its hometown of St. Paul, as well as to clients throughout the world.

During World War II, Northwest Airlines chose Ellerbe to plan its facilities at the St. Paul Municipal Airport. Ellerbe built the first building for 3M and the first Mayo Clinic group practice building. And in downtown Minneapolis, the 30-story high-rise known as LaSalle Plaza was designed and built by the firm, and houses its largest office.

Today, Ellerbe Becket offers services ranging from planning, architecture, engineering, interiors, and construction to corporations, developers, government entities, health care organizations, educational institutions, and professional sports franchises.

Ellerbe Becket has won numerous design awards over the course of some 90 years. In the last decade alone, the firm has received more than 200 awards for design, engineering, and construction services. The awards have come from prestigious organizations such as the American Institute of Architects and the American Society of Interior Designers, as well as key industry trade magazines such as *Architecture*, *Engineering News Record*, and *Building Design and Construction*.

THE DESIGN, ENGINEERING, AND CONSTRUCTION EXPERTISE OF ELLERBE BECKET IS EVIDENT IN THE CONTEMPORARY RESORT HOTEL AT WALT DISNEY WORLD IN ORLANDO (TOP) AS WELL AS THE NOTRE DAME MAIN ADMINISTRATION BUILDING IN SOUTH BEND, INDIANA (BOTTOM).

A FOUNDATION IN ST. PAUL

Ellerbe opened for business in borrowed drafting space in St. Paul. His first major project was the Old Fireside Inn, a combined dance hall, retail store, and apartment complex in St. Paul. In 1911, just two years after starting his architectural design firm, Ellerbe brought in Olin Round as his partner. By the end of 1912, Ellerbe & Round had grown to 18 employees.

After his father's death in 1921, Thomas Ellerbe presided over the company for nearly 50 years. The firm's history of designing buildings based on customer needs and providing integrated services originated with Thomas Ellerbe.

In 1988, Ellerbe Associates acquired Welton Becket Inc., to become Ellerbe Becket. The Welton Becket firm, founded in the mid-1930s, had a reputation for highly creative designs and interesting clientele. Founder Welton Becket moved in Hollywood circles, and designed houses for movie stars such as James Cagney and Cesar Romero. Becket's firm had notable commissions including Century City, Capitol Records, and five hotels for Walt Disney World in Florida.

INTEGRATED SERVICES

By the mid-1990s, Ellerbe Becket was one of the oldest and largest design firms in America, but Bob Degenhardt, professional engineer and CEO, says there was something missing.

"Customers were becoming increasingly disenchanted with the process of getting buildings designed and constructed," says Degenhardt. "We set out to reinvent the industry by creating true collaboration with the firm's clients and stakeholders on every project."

As a result, Ellerbe Becket has taken the lead in this industry trend back to the time-honored tradition of the master builder. The firm takes full responsibility for the entire continuum of each project. This approach, which Ellerbe Becket calls integrated services, means that the best design and construction team works together from the start, resulting in a high level of creativity

and control for the client, as well as for the employees working on the project.

ELLERBE INNOVATIONS

Throughout its long history, Ellerbe Becket has always been known as an innovator, ready to explore and discover new ideas and to act on them after diligent research and analysis. For instance, in 1922, Thomas Ellerbe proposed a radical new approach to hospital design—equipping each room with a private bathroom.

During World War II, structural steel became scarce. Ellerbe engineers devised an innovative solution for a new Northwest Airlines hangar at St. Paul Municipal Airport: the largest laminated pine arch-trusses ever fabricated, spanning the 170-foot width of the hangar.

By the mid-1990s, Ellerbe Becket had pioneered another health care breakthrough: wellness centers. This dynamic, new approach to maintaining a patient's health combines preventive medicine, complementary medicine, fitness, and social interaction under one roof.

On the technology side, the Ellerbe Becket-designed Bank One Ballpark in Phoenix was the first such facility in the world with a retractable roof and natural grass. The ballpark, home to Major League Baseball's Arizona Diamondbacks, opened in 1998.

And the new Science Museum of Minnesota, which opened on the banks of the Mississippi River in St. Paul in 1999, has the first convertible dome IMAX theater in North America. Giant mechanical arms rotate the screen from a nine-story flat screen to a nine-story domed screen, giving the museum flexibility to use either format.

To this day, Ellerbe Becket remains an innovator. For example, in designing and constructing the new E*TRADE Regional Operations Center in Atlanta, Ellerbe Becket threw the traditional building timeline out the window, and delivered the state-of-the-art, 165,000-square-foot computer command center for financial and stock trading operations in just 11 months.

Ellerbe Becket also believes in internal innovation. Thomas Ellerbe was a leader in the cooperative movement and initiated many innovative management concepts. Ellerbe was the first large firm to pay salaries and provide employee benefits, and the first to experiment with a four-day workweek.

The simple formula of innovation and teamwork will continue to fuel the firm's success. A growing list of notable projects and a focus on professionalism and integrity help Ellerbe Becket remain poised for growth and expansion, whatever time and technology may bring, in the years to come.

AMONG THE INNOVATIVE AND ACCLAIMED PROJECTS OF ELLERBE BECKET ARE (CLOCKWISE FROM TOP LEFT) LOS ANGELES INTERNATIONAL AIRPORT THEME BUILDING; SAITAMA SUPER ARENA, SAITAMA, JAPAN; SCIENCE MUSUEM OF MINNESOTA, ST. PAUL; KINDGOM CENTRE, RIYADH, SAUDI ARABIA.

FOUNDED IN 1903 AS A SMALL WOOD WINDOW FRAME MANUFACTURING business by Danish immigrant Hans Andersen and his two sons, Andersen Corporation is now the foremost worldwide manufacturer of wood windows and patio doors. The privately held company employs approximately 6,000 people and operates a more than 2.5

FROM TOP:
ANDERSEN WAS FOUNDED AS ANDERSEN LUMBER COMPANY IN HUDSON, WISCONSIN, IN 1903, AND MOVED TO SOUTH STILLWATER (NOW BAYPORT), MINNESOTA, IN 1913.

ANDERSEN PERMA-SHIELD® VINYL CLADDING COUPLED WITH ADVANCED INSULATING GLASS, ELIMINATED THE NEED FOR STORM WINDOWS AND, IN 1966, LAUNCHED CLAD WOOD AS A NEW CATEGORY IN THE WINDOW INDUSTRY.

FOR REMODELING AND NEW CONSTRUCTION PROJECTS, THE ANDERSEN WEB SITE—WWW.ANDERSENWINDOWS.COM—PROVIDES CONSUMERS WITH A WEALTH OF INFORMATION.

million-square-foot manufacturing and office facility along the St. Croix River.

Hans Andersen pledged from the beginning that his company would be "different and better." This motto has held true over the years; the company to this day is known for its innovations and excellence in window manufacture and design, as well as for its commitment to customer satisfaction, its protection of the environment, and its employees.

CHANGING THE WAY AMERICA SEES WINDOWS

Andersen Corporation has been instrumental in changing the look and design of American homes. The company's first innovation, the 10-minute window, was assembled quickly from standardized horizontal and vertical frame pieces available in several sizes, with no time-consuming cutting or trimming necessary. This groundbreaking assembly method allowed mass production of window and door frames, which Andersen began in 1904—nine years ahead of Henry Ford's assembly line for automobiles. Working together on Andersen's assembly

line, his 12 employees could produce 120 frames daily, helping the business break even just two years after opening.

Throughout the 1930s and 1940s, Andersen Corporation continued to advance the industry with products such as Pressure Seal weather stripping, which eliminated the need for metal on window frames. The Andersen Master Casement window was the first completely assembled window unit—including sash, frame, and hardware—in the industry. Andersen Windowalls®, trademarked in 1944, offered a dramatic new design feature that significantly opened the home to outdoor beauty and light. Also, the Andersen Gliding Window brought a contemporary twist to American homes.

The Flexivent® window, which could be installed to open in, out, or sideways, further revolutionized the industry. Introduced in 1952, it spurred the fastest buildup of production capacity the Andersen plant had ever experienced. Thanks to the Flexivent, the company doubled its share of the window business in just two years.

More recently, Andersen has introduced new window materials that not only make durable and beautiful windows, but also demonstrate the company's commitment to the environment. For instance, Fibrex® material is a composite made of reclaimed wood fiber from Andersen manu-

facturing operations and vinyl. Fibrex material is as strong and stable as wood, but requires less maintenance. Using this material for window and door frames helps conserve raw timber and reduces solid waste. The company also developed Andersen High-Performance™ insulating glass to help keep heat inside buildings in the winter and outside in the summer.

In addition to its use of innovative materials, Andersen is actively working to reduce the effect of its manufacturing processes on the environment. Since 1988, Andersen has cut its hazardous chemical emissions by more than 95 percent and its volatile organic compounds by more than 50 percent. The company also has reduced landfill deposits by 98 percent.

Andersen has been recognized for its environmentally responsible manufacturing methods with pollution prevention awards from the State of Minnesota and the Minnesota Chamber of Commerce. Nationally, the company has received the Alliance to Save Energy's prestigious Stars of Energy Efficiency award.

SATISFIED CUSTOMERS THROUGH SATISFIED EMPLOYEES

Complete customer satisfaction has always been an overarching goal at Andersen Corporation. To help ensure satisfied customers,

the company works to ensure satisfied employees. As early as 1914, Andersen pioneered a new path in employee relations by introducing profit sharing.

When Hans Andersen's son Fred took over the business, he continued his father's legacy with disability insurance, paid vacations, thrift bonuses, and other savings incentives. Many of those who work at Andersen today are third- and fourth-generation employees.

To encourage employees to share their ideas for improvement, beginning in 1924, Andersen paid $2 to any employee whose idea was implemented by the company. Since then, tens of thousands of dollars have been awarded for ideas that save the company time, money, or material, or that improve safety, products, or production.

SERVING A BROAD SPECTRUM

A ndersen Corporation serves a broad spectrum of customers in both residential and commercial market segments, from home owners, remodelers, and builders to commercial building owners and architects. The company's direct export sales are growing, and its international markets currently include North America, South America, Europe, Asia, and the Middle East.

In the United States, residential window replacement is growing

rapidly as the housing stock ages. In response to home owner preference, Andersen developed Renewal by Andersen® products, which offer home owners quality windows made from Fibrex material to replace existing older windows. Renewal by Andersen provides a complete buying experience from assessing the home owner's window needs, to producing windows to fit specific openings, to complete installation.

Andersen serves not only the marketplace, but also the community with donations of time, money, and product. The company's primary focus locally and nationally is affordable housing. To date, Habitat for Humanity has been the beneficiary of a significant

amount of Andersen support, including nearly $1.5 million in windows over a five-year period and thousands of volunteer hours building houses. Additionally, Andersen assists a variety of community activities that support architecture and design, including the Minnesota Children's Museum and the Walker Art Center. The company also supports the advancement of the building industry in its corporate giving through scholarships and other activities.

Through innovation, commitment to customer satisfaction, environmental stewardship, and community service, Andersen Corporation continues the legacy of being "different and better."

CLOCKWISE FROM TOP LEFT: VOLUNTEERS FROM ANDERSEN CORPORATION AND RENEWAL BY ANDERSEN BUILD HOMES FOR HABITAT FOR HUMANITY. IN 1999, MORE THAN 2,700 VOLUNTEER HOURS WERE DONATED TO HOMES LIKE THIS ONE ON THE EAST SIDE OF ST. PAUL.

ANDERSEN'S CLAD-WOOD WINDOWS HAVE WIDE APPLICATION IN LIGHT COMMERCIAL BUILDING.

RENEWAL BY ANDERSEN MOVED INTO ITS STRIKING, NEW, 227,000-SQUARE-FOOT HEADQUARTERS AND FABRICATION FACILITY IN COTTAGE GROVE IN JUNE 1999.

BETHEL COLLEGE & SEMINARY HAS BEEN SERVING THE MIDWEST FOR NEARLY 130 years and has been an integral part of the St. Paul community for nearly a century. Today, the 243-acre, wooded campus on Lake Valentine is home to a four-year liberal arts college, a seminary, and a graduate and continuing education center. Known for its academic excellence, Bethel

has an overarching mission of graduating men and women whose academic preparation, spiritual maturity, and broad Christian vision give them exceptional leadership potential.

THE HISTORY

Bethel has evolved from a school for dissenting Swedish Baptist immigrants into an educational institution for today's broader evangelical world. The college and seminary are a ministry of the churches of the Baptist General Conference.

The roots of the school and seminary are tightly interwoven with the *läsare* movement in Scandinavia. *Läsare* is a Swedish term used to describe the efforts of revivalists going from house to house, reading the Scriptures, and urging personal faith in Christ. The movement shares its roots with denominations like the Evangelical Covenant Church and the Evangelical Free Church.

Today, fewer and fewer Bethel students are from Scandinavian backgrounds, and the curriculum is designed to address the needs of a wide range of students of different ethnicities and denominations.

For the 4,000 students who attend Bethel College & Seminary, including approximately 800 stu-

dents in adult programs and another 800 seminary students, that rich heritage reverberates throughout each field of study, ranging from theology to the most high-tech discipline.

BETHEL COLLEGE

Year after year, *U.S. News & World Report* has ranked Bethel College among the top 10 liberal arts colleges in the region. The college offers 67 areas of study with 58 majors. Highly respected in their personal fields, Bethel faculty have an unusual dedication to building personal relationships with their students.

Students are encouraged to broaden their horizons with off-campus study through a myriad of academic exchange programs that

span the globe. The Institute of International Education has ranked Bethel 19th in the nation in the number of students studying overseas.

Closer to home, Bethel students and faculty are known for their community service efforts. Students in Bethel's environmental nursing course, for instance, recently helped to assess the greenspace in the Frogtown area of urban St. Paul. Many Bethel students volunteer on Habitat for Humanity projects, and business faculty and students regularly offer free tax assistance to low-income residents.

Bethel's goal is to inspire students to strive for academic excellence, to grow in godliness, to deepen their understanding of human relationships, and to discover their unique talents and gifts as they explore career possibilities. Spirituality is not considered an add-on or something limited to chapel services. Faith development is woven throughout the very fabric of a Bethel education. For instance, upwards of 3,000 students attend the student-led Sunday night vesper services on campus.

Bethel graduates are highly sought after in the workplace not only for their academic achievements, but also for their maturity, character, and integrity.

BETHEL SEMINARY

Bethel Seminary was founded in 1871 by John Alexis Edgren to train Scandinavian Baptist

BETHEL COLLEGE & SEMINARY, WHICH COMPRISES A FOUR-YEAR LIBERAL ARTS COLLEGE AND SEMINARY, AS WELL AS A GRADUATE AND CONTINUING EDUCATION CENTER, HAS BEEN AN INTEGRAL PART OF THE ST. PAUL COMMUNITY FOR NEARLY A CENTURY.

LEE PROHOFSKY

preachers. Edgren's theological seminary for Scandinavians was originally associated with the University of Chicago, but moved to St. Paul in 1914.

Today, Bethel Seminary reflects Edgren's vision of seminary education as one of "deep piety and hunger for knowing God intimately, intertwined with a profound commitment to excellence in scholarship." The seminary's programs are divided into three centers for learning: the Center for Biblical and Theological Foundations, the Center for Transformational Leadership, and the Center for Spiritual and Personal Formation.

To reach the widest possible audience, Bethel Seminary, which has campuses in St. Paul and San Diego, and offers classes at four East Coast sites, is also in the fore-

front of evangelical distance education. For instance, the Willow Creek Community Church in South Barrington, Illinois, has joined with Bethel Seminary to offer a comprehensive, three-year degree program to provide practical, hands-on training through Willow Creek. The program includes seminary courses through distance education and an intensive, two-week summer course on the St. Paul campus.

THE COMMUNITY

Bethel College & Seminary reaches out to the St. Paul community through a concert series at its 1,700-seat Benson Great Hall, recognized as one of the premier concert venues in the Upper Midwest. Recent series have featured the Saint Paul Chamber Orchestra,

Dale Warland Singers, Cantati Evangelica, and a special musical celebration of Black History Month. Bethel's spacious facilities are also used regularly throughout the year by the Immigration and Naturalization Service to conduct the ceremonies in which several hundred immigrants take their oath of allegiance as new U.S. citizens.

In 1989, Bethel College began PACE—Program in Adult College Education—its adult degree completion program. Today, that program, as well as master's degrees in communication, counseling psychology, nursing, organizational leadership, and education, is offered through Bethel's Center for Graduate and Continuing Studies. The programs are designed to meet the special needs of adult learners, with classes meeting one or two evenings each week. Bethel is also working with area companies to train employees at their work sites. The center also offers one-day seminars open to the entire community on topics ranging from communication and conflict resolution to technology for pastors.

The Bethel campus continues to expand with the development of additional laboratory, studio, and classroom spaces; the construction of a 10-acre athletic complex that is open to the public; and the building of a 270-bed residence hall. These developments reflect Bethel's ongoing efforts to address the needs of 21st-century students and serve the wider community, while maintaining its vision as a vibrant Christian learning community.

BETHEL SEMINARY WAS FOUNDED IN 1871 BY JOHN ALEXIS EDGREN TO TRAIN SCANDINAVIAN BAPTIST PREACHERS.

THE GOAL OF BETHEL COLLEGE IS TO INSPIRE STUDENTS TO STRIVE FOR ACADEMIC EXCELLENCE, TO GROW IN GODLINESS, TO DEEPEN THEIR UNDERSTANDING OF HUMAN RELATIONSHIPS, AND TO DISCOVER THEIR UNIQUE TALENTS AND GIFTS AS THEY EXPLORE CAREER POSSIBILITIES.

XCEL ENERGY INC.

SINCE THE EARLY 1900S, XCEL ENERGY INC., FORMERLY KNOWN AS NORTHERN States Power Company (NSP), has been the premier provider of electricity and natural gas in St. Paul and throughout the Upper Midwest. "One of the reasons St. Paul is a healthy, vibrant place is because for all those years it has had a safe and reliable supply of low-cost energy, produced in an

environmentally responsible manner," says Jim Howard, Xcel Energy chairman. "We work very hard—in all kinds of weather—to produce and deliver energy, and we're going to keep doing that to keep St. Paul strong and growing."

THE ENERGY TO MAKE THINGS BETTER

The story of Xcel Energy and its predecessor companies is closely intertwined with that of the city itself, as well as running parallel to the great technological innovations of the last century. In 1856, five businessmen from St. Paul secured a franchise from the Minnesota legislature to create the St. Paul Gas Light Company to illuminate St. Paul's city streets with gas street lamps. Among that quintet was Alexander Ramsey, the first territorial governor of Minnesota and later the young state's second governor from 1860 to 1863.

It wasn't until 1861 that St. Paul Gas Light actually began lighting the streets, bringing St. Paul the aura of civic respectability that lighted avenues offered at the time. The gas, however, was of poor quality: individual streetlights had to be turned on and off each day, and they posed a fire hazard. A more efficient and safer alternative—electricity— was soon to arrive in St. Paul.

Around 1900, Henry Byllesby arrived in Minnesota from Pennsylvania and began buying small power plants all across the Midwest. In Minnesota, Byllesby organized the Washington County Light and Power Company, bought the Stillwater Gas and Electric Company, and united the two as the Consumer Power Company in 1909. Three years later, he bought the Minneapolis Electric Company, which was just beginning to supply coal-generated power from the new Riverside power plant. The new company created by Byllesby became NSP in 1916.

By the 1920s, NSP was in direct competition with St. Paul Gas. Competition between the companies was so fierce that there were parts of the city that had NSP lines running down one side of the street and St. Paul Gas lines running down the other. Once in a while, fistfights

even broke out between NSP and St. Paul Gas crews.

However, the two rivals eventually became friends when NSP bought St. Paul Gas in 1925. The wave of utility consolidations, ushered in by the technological advancement of transmission line systems in the 1920s, laid the groundwork for the creation of highly centralized utility holding companies. NSP's formation early in the century involved some of the biggest names—like Byllesby—in the national electric utility industry at the time.

By the end of the 1920s, just 1 percent of the utility corporations in the country controlled some 85 percent of the nation's electric generation. These holding companies quickly flourished, and just as quickly disappeared due to political and economic forces.

The Twin Cities were almost fully electrified by the end of the 1920s. For the next decade, NSP would work to bring electricity to the rural areas and the small farms of the Upper Midwest. Electricity brought about a small revolution in life on the farm, making many tasks that had required heavy labor, like pumping water, much easier. In farmhouses and in city homes, electric appliances were bringing

unheard of convenience. Electric stoves, fans, even irons changed the way people went about their daily chores.

As electric use grew, the price of electricity dropped. A kilowatt-hour cost 24 cents in 1881, but cost only six cents in the late 1920s. In 1932, the area's first high-pressure natural gas transmission line went into service. Natural gas was cheaper and cleaner than coal gas, and today it is the only gas Xcel Energy sells.

In the economic boom years after World War II, many people equipped their homes with the latest appliances. NSP's electric sales doubled between 1941 and 1951. Gas sales tripled, and rates continued to drop.

It wasn't until the 1973 OPEC oil embargo that the public once again became conscious of the energy it was consuming. Evolving with the times, NSP studied ways to save energy in homes and businesses, as well as investigating new techniques for generating electricity.

For instance, NSP began working with landfill operators through its subsidiary, NRG, to extract methane from landfills to produce electricity. Refuse-derived fuel is another method the company has found to harness alternative sources of energy.

Through the years, NSP accomplished much to maintain environmental quality by making environmental commitments early and avoiding costly retrofits. For instance, the company invested more than $350 million to reduce sulfur dioxide emissions from fossil-fuel-burning plants. NSP reduced such emissions by nearly 75 percent, while at the same time increasing fossil fuel generation by 51 percent.

PEOPLE POWER

The power that fuels the furnace or makes the coffeepot brew coffee may be invisible to see, but the people behind that power are a visible and most important asset to Xcel Energy. "It's an energy source that is every bit as important as natural gas and electricity," Howard says. "I have long maintained that underlying the dedication of employees is the realization that by producing and delivering energy, we aren't just contributing to quality of life. We're ensuring life itself. Xcel Energy employees recognize this as a sacred obligation, and it motivates them as nothing else could."

Xcel Energy and its employees' commitment to St. Paul go beyond providing energy. The company also supplies powerful corporate funding and energetic volunteers in the community.

As part of the Greening the Great River Park project several years ago, 1,000 NSP volunteers planted 7,000 trees and shrubs at the High Bridge plant along the Mississippi River in St. Paul. This prompted other companies to do the same, and as of 2000, there are 30,000 new trees along the river. As Howard says,

THE STORY OF XCEL ENERGY AND ITS PREDECESSOR COMPANIES IS CLOSELY INTERTWINED WITH THAT OF THE CITY ITSELF, AS WELL AS RUNNING PARALLEL TO THE GREAT TECHNOLOGICAL INNOVATIONS OF THE LAST CENTURY.

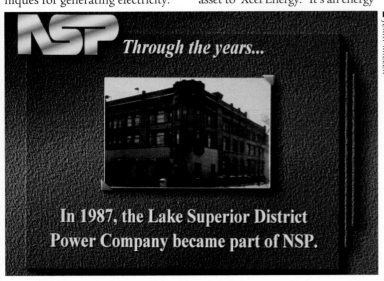

In 1987, the Lake Superior District Power Company became part of NSP.

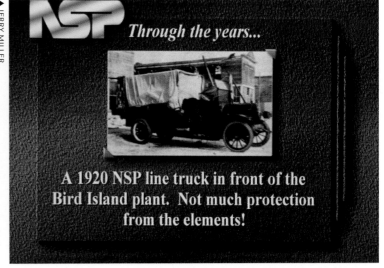

A 1920 NSP line truck in front of the Bird Island plant. Not much protection from the elements!

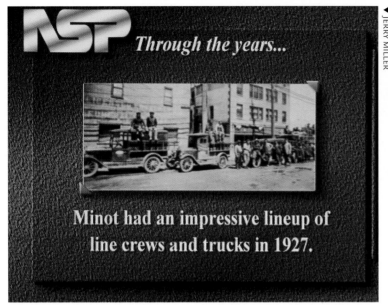

Through the years...

Minot had an impressive lineup of line crews and trucks in 1927.

Through the years...

State-of-the-art hydro turbine (in 1913!). NSP acquired this facility when the company purchased St. Cloud Public Service Company in 1924.

XCEL ENERGY CONTINUES TO EVOLVE WITH TECHNOLOGICAL, POLITICAL, AND ECONOMIC REALITIES OF THE TIMES.

"That's a legacy that will last for generations."

For almost a decade, NSP worked with St. Paul on energy efficiency programs that saved the city about $1.6 million annually. And through the company's corporate contributions program, NSP contributed $1.5 million a year to nonprofit agencies located in St. Paul. Xcel Energy's employees continue to volunteer their time on a regular basis to de-

ON AUGUST 18, 2000, XCEL ENERGY WAS FORMED BY THE MERGER OF DENVER-BASED NEW CENTURY ENERGIES AND NSP.

liver Meals on Wheels, build houses for Habitat for Humanity, and contribute generously to United Way.

NSP donated six aerial spotlights to illuminate the historic Wabasha Street Bridge in downtown St. Paul for special occasions. These lights are 100 times brighter than the lights at an evening baseball game, yet it costs only 99 cents an hour to operate all six of them. "Lighting the bridge was a good way to illus-

trate our longtime presence in St. Paul and our continuing commitment to this great city," Howard says.

READY FOR THE FUTURE

On August 18, 2000, Xcel Energy was formed by the merger of Denver-based New Century Energies and NSP. At the dawn of the new millennium, Xcel Energy provides electricity and natural gas to approximately 3.1 million customers in Arizona, Colorado, Kansas, Michigan, Minnesota, New Mexico, North Dakota, Oklahoma, South Dakota, Texas, Wisconsin, and Wyoming, with operating revenues of $6.9 billion. As it did through the last century, Xcel Energy continues to evolve with the technological, political, and economic realities of the times.

In announcing the merger, Howard told employees that it would "combine two well-managed, mid-continent electric and gas companies in order to provide a strong platform for assuring low-cost, quality service to the region during a time of rapid change in the utility industry." He also assured employees and the community at large that Xcel Energy would remain committed to the city just as NSP had been for nearly a century.

"We can only be as good as the territory in which we operate," Howard says. "We can't pick up our power plants and go somewhere else. We are as much a part of this community as anyone. We have a real stake in the economic well-being of this area."

A FEW YEARS AGO, WHEN THE PARTNERS AT LETHERT, SKWIRA, SCHULTZ & Co. LLP (LSS) were reviewing a draft of the firm's new brochure, they noticed that one of the clients mentioned was also included in the firm's first promotional materials back in 1927. That business was still a client of LSS some 70 years later.

That's not surprising for this firm of certified public accountants and business consultants, where the third generation of Letherts and the second generation of Skwiras are still working, along with other long-term employees, to serve a fourth generation of St. Paul businesses.

"That longevity has helped us retain our people and our clients," says Michael J. Lethert, CPA and partner, whose grandfather, Joseph A. Lethert, founded the firm in 1918.

Specializing in accounting, audits, tax preparation, and business consulting for privately held businesses as well as individuals, LSS prides itself on the personal attention and understanding it can give its clients.

"There is a significant amount of partner involvement in every account," says Gerald M. Faletti, managing partner—who started at LSS as an intern in 1975. "The marketplace wants to treat what we do as a commodity. We see it as a service business. We offer great service at a competitive price."

HELPING BUSINESSES CONDUCT BUSINESS

A native of St. Paul, Joseph A. Lethert opened the Central Accounting Bureau in 1918. His son, Al Lethert, went to work at the family business when he was still in high school. He never retired and worked at the firm until his death. Through the years, several uncles and aunts also became part of the business, which became Lethert, Skwira, Schultz & Co. in 1976.

During the 1930s, Michael Skwira wanted to join the Lethert firm so badly he offered to work for nothing just to get the experience. He got the job and ultimately stayed—becoming a partner—until his retirement. Skwira's son, Michael Skwira Jr., followed in his father's footsteps, just as in the Lethert family, and began working at the firm in the early 1960s.

Today, with eight partners and a total of about 30 employees, the firm continues its tradition of offering personalized service and financial expertise primarily for closely held entrepreneurial businesses. "We have some insight on how to deal with family business," Lethert says.

The core services LSS provides are audits and accounting functions such as preparation of financial statements and books of account. "We become the client's accounting department in some cases," Faletti says. "We do payroll, sales taxes, and business taxes."

The firm also does tax preparation for businesses as well as individuals, and business consulting in such varied areas as profit sharing plans, computerization or networking, cost benefit analysis, and even interviewing comptroller candidates.

Rather than departmentalize each function, LSS assigns one "general practitioner" to each client. This person is the client's main contact at the firm, and he or she can easily consult with specialists among the other firm members as specific questions arise. "We've bucked the trend of departmentalizing," Faletti says. "Our clients seem to like that."

Many clients originally may have come to LSS for tax preparation, yet through the years developed a relationship that includes a whole array of services—from personal estate planning to merger and acquisition advice.

"We get close to our clients," says Faletti. "The people here at Lethert, Skwira, Schultz & Co. LLP genuinely care about other people."

AT LETHERT, SKWIRA, SCHULTZ & CO. LLP, THE PARTNERS AND EMPLOYEES ARE PERSONALLY INVOLVED AND WILLING TO GO THAT EXTRA STEP TO SERVE CLIENTS.

1921-1979

HE JAMES J. HILL GROUP IS A MULTIDISCIPLINARY BUSINESS information center that has developed an international reputation as the home of the business information experts. The centerpiece of the group is the James J. Hill Research Library, a remarkable institution designed to be a complete collection of business information, products, and services.

The Hill Library, which opened in 1921, is more than a historic landmark in downtown St. Paul. With its exhaustive collection of print, CD-ROM, and on-line materials and periodicals on all aspects of business, the library serves as a vibrant source of the most comprehensive information for the business community.

"The Hill Library has always been an important part of the economic development here in St. Paul," says Ann O'Connor, director of Hill Library Services. "Our users include businesspeople, employees, students, and all sorts of entrepreneurs. We have strong ties to local business education organizations as well. James J. Hill was a self-made man eager to offer that opportunity to others. I believe he has done that."

THE DREAM OF AN EMPIRE BUILDER

Hill played a pivotal role in the development of Minnesota and the entire northern tier of states, all the way to the coast of Washington, in large part with his Great Northern Railway. "While his own formal education ended when he was 14, Hill understood its importance; much of his philanthropy was devoted to educational institutions, including establishing St. Paul's first general reference library," says Eileen R. McCormack, associate curator for Hill Manuscript Services. "He believed that reliable, timely information was one of his best business allies."

Pledging $750,000 of his own money, Hill envisioned that the library would provide the answer to any question "from the origins of art to the electric current, from the philosophies of the sages to soap." Although Hill died before his library doors opened, his vision was realized with a comprehensive collection of reference works, excluding only medicine, law, genealogy, and popular fiction.

In the mid-1970s, the library's board of directors decided to narrow the scope from general reference to business research, an area in which the library had always been particularly strong. Today, the Hill Library is one of the nation's largest business resource collections with useful information for start-up businesses as well as multinational conglomerates.

Overall, the library houses approximately 1,000 business and industry-specific periodicals in print, plus hundreds of others available via the Internet. The library also has a special focus on the food industry with extensive specialized publications such as *Pizza Today* and *Pasta Journal*.

The library's staff is trained to guide visitors through the wealth of information to the most valuable materials for them. "We try to help them articulate exactly what they want and then teach them how to use the resources so they leave with the right information," O'Connor says.

For those who would rather have a professional gather and analyze information for their business, the James J. Hill Group provides research and consultative services. The team of business information professionals offers customized consulting, market research, competitive intelligence, consumer insights, industry analysis, and document delivery.

Hill would be pleasantly surprised if he visited his library today. "He was very practical," McCormack says. "If there had been things like business libraries back in his time, this would have been a business library from the start. Actually, I don't think he'd be surprised at all."

THE JAMES J. HILL GROUP PROVIDES UNMATCHED EXPERTISE BY OFFERING A ONE-OF-A-KIND BLEND OF INTELLECTUAL CAPITAL, CONTENT, AND TECHNOLOGY (LEFT).

WITH MORE THAN 800,000 TITLES, THE JAMES J. HILL RESEARCH LIBRARY, THE CENTERPIECE OF THE JAMES J. HILL GROUP, HOUSES AN EXTENSIVE COLLECTION OF BUSINESS RESOURCES (MIDDLE).

EXTENSIVE BACKGROUNDS IN MARKETING RESEARCH, COMPETITIVE INTELLIGENCE, AND CORPORATE DEVELOPMENT SET THE HILL GROUP STAFF APART FROM OTHER BUSINESS RESOURCES (RIGHT).

DAVID ELLIS

DAVID ELLIS

DAVID ELLIS

IN EIGHT DECADES OF EXISTENCE, NEWMECH COMPANIES, INC. HAS helped to shape both St. Paul and the Twin Cities with structures such as the Mall of America, United Hospital, Canterbury Downs, Ordway Center for the Performing Arts, and the majority of the elementary and high schools in the area. The work of this state-of-the-art, diversified

mechanical contracting firm is oftentimes not apparent to the casual observer–since it includes heating, air-conditioning, ventilation, plumbing, and fire protection systems–but such work is critical to any building's success.

Since its founding in 1921, NewMech has steadily added services to become highly diversified and able to serve a variety of both large and small clients with the highest level of expertise and efficiency. With divisions including heating and plumbing, sheet metal fabrication, fire protection, hospital and health care, industrial, spiral pipe, and service/special projects, the NewMech's annual volume today exceeds $80 million, reflecting the company's motto, which clearly states, "Excellence is not our goal–it is our standard."

A COMPLETE CONTRACTOR

NewMech has built a solid reputation as a complete mechanical contractor in the designing and building of health care facilities, including their upgrade and maintenance. The company prides itself on staying abreast of the constant changes and advances in health care technology.

As with all projects undertaken by NewMech, state-of-the-art, computer-aided design and draft-

ing (CADD) equipment and software are used. NewMech employees, who are specially certified to work in health care facilities, use the company's CADD capabilities to lay out and coordinate the most complex equipment and systems with precision and care.

NewMech was involved with design/build/negotiate projects long before this process had become popular in the industry. The design/build/negotiate process allows a client to start a project prior to the completion of the construction documents. Advantages include addressing the owner's needs directly, timely responses to design issues, and a shorter overall project construction time frame. Another distinct advantage is the fact that the same people who negotiate the project supervise the installation and remain through completion.

NewMech's in-house, 60,000-square-foot piping and sheet metal fabrication shops allow the firm's highly skilled employees to fabricate process piping, industrial sheet metal, air handling and ducting, and spiral pipes in the most cost-effective and efficient manner. The pipe fabrication shop contains two 10-ton bridge cranes, submerged arc welding equipment, pipe rollers, positioners, an orbital welder, and a completely computerized

and automated RotoWeld 2000. The sheet metal shop contains state-of-the-art fabrication equipment that keeps NewMech ahead of the industry. NewMech's fabrication services division has worked on projects ranging from microbreweries to clean rooms.

Spiral pipe is another specialty area for NewMech. This pipe is strong and lightweight, has lower installation costs, and offers flexibility in ducting designs. Not only is spiral piping functional, but also exposed spiral pipe is increasingly popular in today's architectural designs.

In each of its projects, NewMech uses a partnering approach that involves working effectively with all parties, including the owners, architects, engineers, and general contractors. This approach offers impressive cost benefits and timely completion.

NewMech also is committed to understanding and meeting a customer's service needs, offering full-coverage, preventive maintenance, as well as customized service agreements backed by 24-hour emergency service. The attitude of the company is evident in two of its philosophical tenets: providing high-quality mechanical services to its clients, and completing projects on schedule and within budget.

NEWMECH COMPANIES, INC. IS COMMITTED TO MEETING A CUSTOMER'S SERVICE NEEDS, OFFERING FULL-COVERAGE, PREVENTIVE MAINTENANCE, AS WELL AS CUSTOMIZED SERVICE AGREEMENTS BACKED BY 24-HOUR EMERGENCY SERVICE (LEFT).

NEWMECH'S IN-HOUSE, 60,000-SQUARE-FOOT PIPING AND SHEET METAL FABRICATION SHOPS ALLOW THE FIRM'S EMPLOYEES TO FABRICATE PROCESS PIPING, INDUSTRIAL SHEET METAL, AIR HANDLING AND DUCTING, AND SPIRAL PIPES (RIGHT).

ANYONE WHO HAS EVER ENJOYED DINNER IN A FINE RESTAURANT, spent a relaxing night in a comfortable hotel room, or quenched his or her thirst with a refreshing soda has most likely experienced firsthand what it means to be Ecolab clean. St. Paul-based Ecolab is the world leader in providing cleaning, sanitation, and service

solutions to businesses in the hospitality, health care, and industrial markets. The company's customers include restaurants and hotels, food and beverage processing plants, health care facilities, schools, dairy farms, vehicle wash operations, and many others.

Ecolab's systems-based organization skillfully unites revolutionary products and services, the most technologically advanced equipment, and comprehensive training and support by a global team of experts ready to serve customers around the clock and around the world.

The company's Circle the Customer-Circle the Globe strategy refers to Ecolab's unique ability to surround its customers with products and services, no matter where or when they do business. In more than 160 countries, Ecolab serves businesses ranging from small, independent establishments to large, high-profile corporations.

For example, Ecolab products work their magic in Walt Disney World, and have even been used to keep the Statue of Liberty looking her best inside and out.

Originally known as Economics Laboratory, the company's beginnings can be traced back to 1923, when it was founded by visionary businessman M.J. Osborn. Anticipating the growth in popularity

of dining outside the home, Osborn— who was working out of his garage— developed Soilax, a chemical detergent for mechanized dish washing.

Today, Ecolab offers an extensive selection of products and programs that meet an ever broadening array of cleaning, sanitation, and service needs. In the United States, the company reaches customers through nine complementary business units: Institutional, Food & Beverage, Pest Elimination, Professional Products, Kay Quick Service Products, Textile Care, Water Care Services, Vehicle Care, and GCS Service. Globally, Ecolab boasts more than 13,000 employees, including a direct sales force totaling nearly 7,000.

Ecolab Center, located at Fifth and Wabasha streets in the heart of downtown St. Paul, serves as the company's world headquarters. The center is also home to Ecolab University, a state-of-the-art, global training facility that helps the company maintain the best-trained sales and service organization in the industry. Ecolab's 24-hour-a-day, seven-day-a-week customer service team, which handles more than 1 million calls each month, is also located in Ecolab Center.

In the neighboring suburbs of Mendota Heights and Eagan, innovation drives Ecolab's future success at the company's world-renowned research, development, and engineering facilities. Ecolab scientists and engineers are continually looking for smarter, better ways to help customers, with more than 400 U.S. patents to prove it.

Throughout its history, Ecolab has defined and redefined clean, all the while protecting its customers' reputations and making the world a safer, more sanitary place to live. Is it clean, or is it Ecolab clean? The difference is the source of Ecolab associates' pride and drives the company's growth.

ECOLAB CENTER, LOCATED AT FIFTH AND WABASHA STREETS IN THE HEART OF DOWNTOWN ST. PAUL, SERVES AS ECOLAB HEADQUARTERS (TOP).

ST. PAUL-BASED ECOLAB IS THE WORLD LEADER IN PROVIDING CLEANING, SANITATION, AND SERVICE SOLUTIONS TO BUSINESSES IN THE HOSPITALITY, HEALTH CARE, AND INDUSTRIAL MARKETS (BOTTOM).

K MSP-TV Channel 9 signed on the air as KEYD on January 9, 1955. Founded by the Family Broadcasting Corporation, the station was owned for a short time in the late 1950s by MGM and held the call letters WMGM. In 1958, WMGM was purchased by Twentieth Century Fox. ▦ During one visit to finalize the deal,

officials from Twentieth Century Fox noticed upon arrival at the Twin Cities airport that their luggage tags were stamped with the Minneapolis/St. Paul airport code MSP. Thus, in 1959, the station was renamed KMSP-TV.

In the early 1960s, KMSP-TV became affiliated with the ABC Network. It carried ABC programming until the fall of 1978, when an affiliate switch in the market gave KMSP-TV its independent station status. The station would remain independent until the fall of 1986, when KMSP-TV took on the newly formed Fox Television Network. KMSP-TV remained a Fox affiliate for two seasons and then reverted to an independent station.

Through the late 1980s and early 1990s, KMSP-TV became one of the strongest independent stations in the country, garnering a higher household share of audience than any other independent television station. KMSP-TV became known for its extensive local programming, such as coverage of Minnesota Twins and Minnesota North Stars hockey games. The station also brought to the Twin Cities the only prime-time newscast at 9 p.m. On January 16, 1995, KMSP-TV helped launch the fifth television network in the area, UPN. KMSP continued making television history as it brought NHL hockey back to Minnesota viewers in the fall of 2000, as the broadcast partner of the Minnesota Wild.

The Future of a Leader

K MSP-TV has always believed that the goal of a television station should be a commitment to the community it serves, and that it can best serve the community with local programming. News and information are a priority at Channel 9. The program 9 News at 9, with anchors Robyne Robinson and Jeff Passolt, has become the news of choice for a growing number of busy viewers who need local

news at a more convenient time. And with a commitment to extend news coverage, KMSP-TV also gives viewers a choice with 9 News at 10, featuring anchors Jeff Passolt and Angela Hampton.

With a goal of providing more local news, KMSP-TV launched Good Day Minnesota in the fall of 1999. This unprecedented, three-and-a-half-hour program now gives Twin Cities viewers a choice for local news in the morning.

In addition to the expansion of its local news coverage, KMSP-TV is using technology to improve its service to the community. The station will be the first full-power digital broadcaster in the Twin Cities. With its digital tower and transmitter already in place, the

station is poised and ready to begin broadcasting digital signals—which provide high-resolution images and CD-quality sound—on Channel 26.

With its continuing commitment to local sports programming, KMSP-TV is the exclusive broadcast home to the Minnesota State High School Hockey and Basketball tournaments. And as professional hockey makes its triumphant return to Minnesota, Channel 9 is the broadcast home of the NHL's newest team, the Minnesota Wild.

With a focus on accurate, up-to-the-minute news coverage, KMSP-TV Channel 9's local roots allow it to innovate and grow to meet the changing needs of its viewers.

KMSP-TV Channel 9's Good Day Minnesota features (from left) Anchor Robin Wolfram, Hosts Tim Sherno and Alix Kendall, and Meteorologist Mike Tsolinas.

Members of KMSP-TV's news team are (from left) Sport Director Jeff Grayson; News Anchors Robyne Robinson, Jeff Passolt, and Angela Hampton; and Meteorologist Sam Scaman.

S INCE 1927, NORTHWEST AIRLINES HAS BEEN SYNONYMOUS WITH AIR travel in St. Paul. In July of that year, the airline counted its first ticketed passenger, St. Paul businessman Byron Webster. He paid $40 for a 12 1/2-hour, one-way flight from the Twin Cities to Chicago via La Crosse, Madison, and Milwaukee. Charlie "Speed" Holman,

Northwest's first pilot, was at the controls.

Northwest has come a long way since it first took to the sky, carrying airmail from the Twin Cities to Chicago with a fleet of two rented, open-cockpit biplanes— a Thomas-Morse Scout and a Curtiss Oriole. Today, with St. Paul and Minneapolis as its world headquarters, as well as a major hub, Northwest is the world's fourth-largest airline, providing 2,600 flights daily on some 400 aircraft to 250 destinations worldwide. And Webster might be surprised to know that the current flight from St. Paul to Chicago on Northwest is nonstop and takes just under an hour.

THE HUB ADVANTAGE

Although the hub-and-spoke system, which was developed after the government deregulated the airline industry in the late 1970s, has come under criticism, St. Paul residents, as well as many local businesses, enjoy the many advantages of the city's status as a Northwest Airlines hub. Northwest routes many of its flights from smaller towns through the Twin Cities hub in order to be more cost effective.

For instance, if three people in Fargo want to fly to Boston on a certain day, it is likely they will fly first to the Twin Cities to board a plane with perhaps 200 other people going to Boston. This procedure is more efficient for the airlines since it doesn't have to fly just three people from Fargo to Boston, and it makes more sense for the passengers since they will have a wider choice of flights from the larger airport.

For those who live in the hub city, travel is extremely convenient. Because they usually don't need to make connecting flights, Twin Cities passengers can fly nonstop from St. Paul to their destinations. Businesses benefit because they have a greater choice of nonstop flights, so their employees do not need to waste precious time changing planes.

HUB-CITY BUSINESSES

A recent study by George Washington University Professor Darryl Jenkins and Northwestern University Professor Robert Gordon states, "Businesses and business travelers tend to be disproportionately located in hub cities." While conducting their research, the professors had unrestricted access to Northwest's proprietary fare and flight information in order to determine objectively whether those living in a hub city pay higher prices—what has been called a "hub premium."

The researchers chose St. Paul because some have claimed that this hub premium is particularly large in the city, where Northwest has 62 percent of the originating and destination traffic. The report discovered, however, that "the

Today, with Minneapolis and St. Paul as its world headquarters, Northwest Airlines is the world's fourth-largest airline.

NORTHWEST PROVIDES 2,600 FLIGHTS DAILY ON SOME 400 AIRCRAFT TO 250 DESTINATIONS WORLDWIDE.

so-called 'hub premium' is a myth," and actually determined that "residents of Northwest's hubs enjoyed a modest discount of about 4 percent when length of trip and major fare categories were held constant."

GOOD FOR BUSINESS

The economic advantage of being a hub city goes beyond the convenience to residents and individual businesses. It also helps attract new business. A recent study by the Aviation Policy Program at George Mason University's Institute of Public Policy concluded that "hub airports act as magnets for high-technology jobs. Proximity to an airport hub has important structural advantages for a local

economy. The evidence shows that a hub airport is a stimulus for high-technology jobs and long-term economic development in a region."

Authored by Kenneth Button and Roger Stough, the Aviation Policy Program's study found that, on average, a hub airport increases a region's high-technology employment by more than 12,000 jobs. The attraction to businesses includes more domestic and international destinations, more structured service through banks of flights, and more frequent same-day return trips. These advantages allow businesses to reduce the generalized costs associated with lengthy air travel time, hotel costs, and time spent in airport terminals. "There

are good reasons to anticipate that the generalized costs of business travel from hub airports is lower than from non-hubs," the report concluded.

All these benefits are in addition to the direct economic stimulation that Northwest provides. In 1999, for example, the airline spent more than $2.6 billion in Minnesota for wages and benefits, goods and services, and government fees and taxes. Some 21,000 Minnesotans are employed by Northwest, including 19,500 in the Twin Cities region centered around St. Paul. As a result, it's no surprise that Northwest has the largest private payroll in the state.

The benefits of direct economic activity, the ability to attract new businesses to St. Paul, and the greater convenience offered to the existing business community make it easy to see why being a hub is good for business and good for travelers. Little did that first paying passenger back in 1927 know what an airline could do for his city.

SINCE 1927, NORTHWEST AIRLINES HAS BEEN SYNONYMOUS WITH AIR TRAVEL IN ST. PAUL.

OLORFUL BRAND MARKS AND AWARD-WINNING, UNUSUAL-SHAPED BUILDINGS are uncommon in financial companies. However, at Fortis, a global family of diversified financial companies, they're the norm. They're part of an innovative, caring company that is solid and straightforward. Fortis, a Dutch/Belgian company, is committed to serving customers

through a worldwide group of more than 200 flexible, locally directed operating companies. The firm is one of the world's largest diversified financial corporations. Fortis is a solid partner offering flexible solutions—a reliable global organization with a local presence.

The Fortis brand mark—which is a combination of the symbol, the word Fortis, and the promise to its customers: "solid partners, flexible solutions"—reflects the diversity of the company's markets, clients, and communities. An Asian folktale underlies this brand mark: The

village is rich because of its pond. Daily life is centered around the pond, which provides water to wash, to drink, to live. The fish also prosper in the pond and provide food for all; thus, the pond is the provider of riches, the fruit of life and prosperity.

Fortis' worldwide businesses, specializing in banking, investments, and specialty insurance, parallel the tale of this pond, the provider of riches. Fortis is a provider of resources that help clients live, grow, develop, and realize their goals. Fortis brings this brand promise alive each day, around the world.

In St. Paul, Fortis is represented by Fortis Financial Group (FFG) and Fortis, Inc. Information Technology, headquartered in Woodbury, an eastern suburb. Fortis Information Technology group provides world-class technology support for Fortis' U.S. companies. Fortis Financial Group is focused on simplifying people's financial lives. To achieve this vision, Fortis lives its brand promise: solid partners, flexible solutions.

SOLID PARTNERS FOR ITS FINANCIAL ADVISERS AND THEIR CUSTOMERS

Fortis Financial Group's mission is to build, distribute, and support financial tools that are simple to buy, simple to sell, and result in the best solutions for customers. The company's core products—variable universal life insurance, variable annuities, and mutual funds—provide options to help meet financial needs during a variety of life stages, and allow customers and their financial advisers to build a portfolio of investments designed to meet those individual needs. Fortis' products are distributed through a national network of independent financial advisers dedicated to simplifying the financial lives of clients. Customer service leadership and a policy of being easy to do business with form the foundation that allows Fortis to be a solid partner with flexible solutions for financial advisers and their clients.

FFG and its predecessor companies have been providing professional money management services in St. Paul since 1949. FFG's predecessors established the first mutual fund in the state of Minnesota. In 1968, the St. Paul Companies acquired what would become the core operations of FFG, and began to operate these businesses under a single head. Fortis acquired FFG as part of the Western Life Insurance Group purchase in 1985.

FORTIS, A DUTCH/BELGIAN COMPANY, IS A SOLID PARTNER OFFERING FLEXIBLE SOLUTIONS—A RELIABLE GLOBAL ORGANIZATION WITH A LOCAL PRESENCE.

In St. Paul, Fortis is represented by Fortis Financial Group (FFG) and Fortis, Inc. Information Technology, headquartered in Woodbury, an eastern suburb.

SOLID PARTNERS TO ITS COMMUNITY

Everyone benefits from a strong community. As a result, Fortis is a key contributor to its local communities, linking employees' time and talents to community needs, providing financial support, and encouraging employees to volunteer. These community initiatives underlie Fortis' guiding values—common sense, common decency, and accountability—which lead to uncommon thinking and uncommon results.

Fortis partners with community-based organizations in a variety of programs designed to increase self-sufficiency of individuals at all stages of their lives. Community involvement programs concentrate in the areas of education, health and human services, quality of life, and diversity. Whether employees are helping students understand the stock market, donating business clothes to assist people reentering the workforce, biking to raise money for health-related research, mentoring diverse students to develop work skills and competencies, or

delivering meals to senior citizens, their efforts focus on helping people help themselves and realize their potential.

SOLID PARTNERS WITH ITS EMPLOYEES

A firm that closely touches its customers' financial lives, Fortis understands first that the company is its people. Highly trained employees are critical to its business success. A caring and innovative employer, Fortis creates a work environment that stimulates growth, rewards and recognizes team and individual contributions, and pro-

vides for the overall well-being of employees.

To foster growth and remain competitive, Fortis offers its employees tuition reimbursement, an annual development week, management and personal development training classes, and an on-site MBA program through the University of St. Thomas. A corporate library and individual career and development planning services augment career development.

The work-life balance program offers flexible work scheduling, on-site child care database resources, telecommuting options where feasible, and wellness programming. In-house sessions on yoga, massage, monthly health-related topics, CPR training, and weight management are provided. Through these programs, Fortis fosters the physical as well as mental well-being of its employees, understanding the importance of helping employees balance their personal and work lives.

Fortis is more than a financial services company. It's a solid partner with its customers, its community, and its employees.

Ericksen Ellison and Associates Inc.

PERCHED ON A BLUFF ABOVE THE MISSISSIPPI RIVER ON THE UNIVERSITY OF Minnesota (U of M) campus sits a structure with unlikely angles and curves that, from a distance, looks like a huge stainless steel sculpture. This eye-catching building—the Frederick R. Weisman Art Museum—was designed by internationally acclaimed California architect Frank O. Gehry.

To engineer the complex climate controls and lighting to protect the artwork, while providing lighting for visitors, the university called on the expertise of the St. Paul engineering firm of Ericksen Ellison and Associates Inc. (EEA).

"Our weather is drastically different from the moderate climate the architect was used to," says Jim Art, PE, EEA vice president. "We worked with them, contributing local know-how, and helped to integrate this into the overall building design."

EEA was formed in St. Paul in 1954 by Leif Ericksen, PE, and George Ellison, PE, for the purpose of practicing mechanical and electrical engineering design. Their early experience was primarily medical, educational, and industrial/commercial buildings. In the 1960s, emphasis was placed on pursuing engineering projects directly with architects, owners, and other consulting engineers. EEA became active in airport facility design, high-tech clean rooms, and computer centers.

ERICKSEN ELLISON AND ASSOCIATES INC. (EEA) WAS FORMED IN ST. PAUL IN 1954 BY LEIF ERICKSEN (LEFT) AND GEORGE ELLISON FOR THE PURPOSE OF PRACTICING MECHANICAL AND ELECTRICAL ENGINEERING DESIGN.

EEA'S UNIQUE EXPERTISE IS EVIDENT IN ITS WORK WITH THE COMPLEX CLIMATE CONTROLS AND LIGHTING FOR THE FREDERICK R. WEISMAN ART MUSEUM AT THE UNIVERSITY OF MINNESOTA.

Bruce Johnson, PE, recently retired president of EEA, succeeded Ericksen in 1985. "What has made EEA a successful company is its devotion to quality and integrity, initiated by its founders, which will lead the new generation of management to future success," says Johnson.

Steady growth throughout the years has resulted in the company's ability to offer services including surveys, facility reports, energy audits, fire protection, security, and communication systems for new construction, as well as remodeling and renovation projects.

ENGINEERED TO SERVE PEOPLE

EEA engineers pride themselves on being able to look beyond their technical expertise to understand how the engineering and design of a building can best serve the people using it. "It is often the nontechnical, human issues that require sensitive and creative problem solving," says President Bill Thiesse, PE.

"Because EEA understands the engineering requirements for the St. Paul area—the regulations, the customs, the work ethic, and the labor traditions—as well as the technical dictates, it is consistently chosen to engineer projects where budget management is crucial, or projects that are high profile and logistically complex," says Thiesse.

From preschools to universities,

from libraries to museums, and from correctional institutions to judicial complexes, EEA has a reputation for first-class creativity and precision in its work. This expertise has led the firm into some unusual projects, including one a half-mile below the surface of the earth.

EEA is designing the lighting and power supply, fire protection, ventilation, and cooling system for the Soudan Underground Research Site in northern Minnesota. "What makes this one of the most interesting projects I have worked on," says Todd Peterson, PE, "is that everything must be brought in through an elevator. It's amazing how they can construct this state-of-the-art facility so far underground."

Closer to home, and well above ground, EEA engineered the sophisticated mechanical, electrical, and communication systems in the Minnesota World Trade Center, located in downtown St. Paul. At the Minnesota Judicial Center, EEA designed the heating and cooling systems, as well as the high-speed electronic data transfer, voice communications, security, and building management systems that connect it to the rest of the Minnesota State Capitol complex.

ENGINEERING FOR EDUCATION

EEA's involvement at St. Paul's Macalester College, Hamline University, Bethel College, College

◄ © 1993 DON F. WONG

of St. Catherine, College of St. Thomas, Northwestern College, St. Paul Technical College, and U of M includes campus activity centers, classrooms and labs, libraries and technology centers, food service facilities, and campus housing.

Working with the Boston architectural firm of Shepley Bullfinch Richardson and Abbott, EEA provided engineering services to Macalester's $12 million, multi-purpose campus center. For the engineering work done on the college's heating and cooling central physical plant, EEA won the 1998 Minnesota Consulting Engineers Council Honor Award.

Besides the Weisman museum, EEA has worked on other unique projects at the U of M. Major renovations at the Walter Digital Technology Center, Folwell Hall, and Coffman Memorial Union presented challenges of bringing historic buildings into the 21st century by incorporating state-of-the-art communications systems, while retaining each building's existing character.

EEA's knowledge of obscure university building codes helped prevent design conflicts while working on the McNamara Alumni Center, U of M Gateway, with renowned architect Antoine Predock.

The U of M chose EEA to take on the engineering demands of the Elmer L. Andersen Library, which houses the Minnesota Library Access Center. Situated 60 feet below ground, this large cavern facility was built to house the university's various archival collections. "There are unique implications for human safety and archive protection," says Art, the project's lead mechanical design engineer. "Many of these are related to fire and smoke, and designing the detection, suppression, and containment systems is very specialized."

EEA is committed to making sure its designs perform as intended, and offers commissioning and training services to ensure that a system engineered by EEA is less costly to maintain and meets energy and operational efficiency goals.

As EEA's philosophy affirms, "We believe in the future. We know that what we design must work as well tomorrow as it does today."

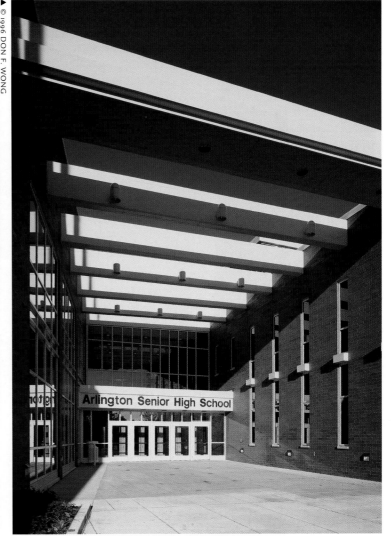

Arlington Senior High School

AERO SYSTEMS ENGINEERING, INC.

AERO SYSTEMS ENGINEERING, INC. (ASE) IS A WORLDWIDE LEADER engaged in the design, manufacture, and construction of jet engine and engine accessory test equipment and facilities, wind tunnels, and other aero-dynamic test facilities for the international marketplace. ▨ ASE's customers include aircraft jet engine and gas

turbine manufacturers; airlines, overhaul, and governmental agencies; and airframe manufacturers. ASE also owns and operates the FluiDyne Aerotest Laboratory, a world-class aerodynamic wind tunnel test facility located in Plymouth, Minnesota.

ASE's home office is located in St. Paul. The company also maintains regional service centers in Cleveland, Ohio; Hampton; Singapore; and Brussels. ASE is committed to providing its customers with comprehensive aftermarket support and the ASE staff is prepared to provide its customers with on-site support anywhere in the world, literally within a matter of hours.

ASE's professional staff includes world-class experts in acoustics, aerodynamics, controls, and data systems, to name just a few key areas. The company has several disciplines, which consult with each other on an ongoing basis, and employees are available to contribute to any project as the need arises. ASE's customers benefit significantly from this synergistic exchange of information.

A NEW CHAPTER IN AVIATION

When ASE was founded in 1967, the aviation world was unveiling a huge new aircraft, the Boeing 747. Equally innovative was the aircraft's engine, the PWA JT9D. With its nearly eight-foot-diameter fan, 5-to-1 bypass ratio, and 45,000

pounds of thrust, this engine opened a new chapter in aviation, as well as a new class of engine test cells—and helped to open the doors of a new test cell company, ASE.

Since then, ASE has introduced new engineering technologies and products to the commercial test cell and wind tunnel markets. In addition, the company pioneered widespread use of the monorail-entry test cell and thrust stand, the cantilever-spring rate adapter concept, the electronic throttle, automatic coupling plates, test cell data acquisition systems, and air-cooled augmenters for afterburning engines.

With the acquisition of the wind tunnel assets of FluiDyne Engineering Corporation in 1993, and the integration of the FluiDyne staff, ASE actively entered two new market areas—wind tunnels and aerotest services. FluiDyne, which has been engaged in these business areas for more than 40 years, is widely recognized as a world leader in wind tunnel design/build and aerotest services.

The staff of ASE is prepared to meet the challenges of today's engine and wind tunnel technologies and their related complexities. The

THE HOME OFFICES OF AERO SYSTEMS ENGINEERING, INC. (ASE) ARE LOCATED IN ST. PAUL (TOP).

ASE TEST EQUIPMENT IS USED TO TEST AFTERBURNING ENGINES THAT POWER THE BOEING F/A-18 AIRCRAFT (BOTTOM).

company's reputation for quality performance, safety, reliability, and productivity has been hard earned, and is widely appreciated by the firm's base of satisfied customers.

ASE is an ISO 9001 registered company, and its employees are committed to meeting global ISO standards.

DIVERSIFIED BUSINESS LINES

As ASE has grown through the years, it now encompasses three lines of business: test cells, wind tunnels, and the aerotest lab.

ASE has been a world leader in turbine engine test cells for more than 30 years. In that time, the company has earned the confidence of major engine manufacturers, airlines, defense organizations, and overhaul agencies around the world. From the beginning, ASE has accomplished this by dedicating itself to meeting each customer's needs. The firm specializes in designs and equipment that reduce engine-handling time and overall test cost, as well as providing complete test cell solutions, including facility design and construction, acoustics, instrumentation, control systems, and test adapter kits.

ASE provides complete design and turnkey design/build services for wind tunnels and specialized environmental/aerodynamic test facilities used by aerospace and associated industries. These services include ongoing engineering task-order contracts with government agencies, such as NASA, in addition to new test facilities, or modernization or automation of existing test complexes. With more than 40 years of experience, ASE is widely regarded as a world leader in the design, construction, and commissioning of wind tunnels and wind tunnel subsystems.

ASE's FluiDyne Aerotest Laboratory provides a complete hardware and testing package tailored to the program needs of the company's customers. The lab's model design, fabrication, and testing capabilities enable ASE's customers to determine engine performance by using scale models to simulate the engine inlet, mixer, pylon, thrust reverser, and exhaust nozzle components.

Ten active test facilities are available at ASE's laboratory. Custom test-facility installations can be provided as well. High-pressure and high-temperature air is available to conduct a variety of aerodynamic studies.

Looking toward the future, Aero Systems Engineering, Inc. will maintain its focus on quality and innovation.

CLOCKWISE FROM LEFT: ASE-FLUIDYNE DESIGNED AND BUILT THE LARGE TRANSONIC WIND TUNNEL USED TO TEST AIRCRAFT MODELS.

THE COMPANY SIMULATED AN ENGINE EXHAUST NOZZLE SYSTEM USING A 10 PERCENT SCALE MODEL.

ASE'S FLUIDYNE AEROTEST LABORATORY IS LOCATED IN PLYMOUTH, MINNESOTA.

UNITED HOSPITAL

United Hospital, the largest hospital in the Twin Cities' east metro area, serves more than 100,000 people each year by providing the full spectrum of health care services—from general care to maternity to major cardiac or brain surgery. "No matter what your health care needs are, we strive to meet them," says Barbara Balik, president of United Hospital.

The hospital is highly regarded for its excellent clinical care in part because its state-of-the-art technology and modern facilities attract some of the most renowned and innovative practitioners in the country. The entire staff is committed to a patient-centered approach that takes into account not only the needs of the patient, but also those of his or her family. More than 90 percent of patients surveyed are satisfied with their experience at United Hospital.

The hospital's foundation lies with several respected St. Paul institutions. United was formed in 1972 when St. Luke's, which was founded in 1855, and the Charles T. Miller Hospital, which was established in 1916, merged. In 1980, West Side's Riverview Memorial Hospital joined the union. Each organization brought its own traditions and specialties to the merger to form a strong, comprehensive care facility. Today, United is a member of the Allina Health System, a nonprofit network of hospitals, clinics, and other health care services.

THE FULL SPECTRUM OF SERVICES

United is, for many, a hospital for life. Beginning with the Birth Center, United offers a complete range of maternity services to women with uncomplicated pregnancies, and to those with high-risk pregnancies. A unique partnership with adjoining Children's Hospitals and Clinics means that specialists and the neonatal intensive care unit are just a few steps away, should a newborn need immediate medical attention. "If you do need a higher level of service, it's comforting to know it's there," Balik says.

In keeping with its philosophy of family-centered care, the Birth Center offers an extensive prenatal and parent education program to help families prepare for the birth of their child and for the parenting that follows. Other specialized services offered by the Birth Center include genetic testing and diagnosis, the Pregnancy and Diabetes Clinic, and the Breastfeeding Resource Center.

The new, state-of-the-art John Nasseff Heart Hospital also illustrates the responsiveness and holistic approach United takes with its patients. This newest addition to United is Minnesota's first heart hospital within a hospital—a response to the growing needs of an aging population. From 1992 to 1997, the number of cardiac procedures performed at United increased 33 percent. The new heart hospital will allow United to grow with the increased need for heart treatment.

This new specialty hospital, which opened in the summer of 2000, is dedicated solely to the diagnosis, treatment, and prevention of heart disease. Supported by a team of experienced staff and physicians, heart hospital patients have access to all the services and programs United provides. The John Nasseff Heart Hospital—a cooperative effort of United, the St. Paul Heart Clinic, and the United Hospital Foundation—provides more effective and efficient services with improved outcomes for patients.

The heart hospital is named after longtime St. Paul resident John Nasseff, whose generous donation supported its construction.

As the largest hospital in the Twin Cities' east metro area, United Hospital serves more than 100,000 people each year by providing the full spectrum of health care services.

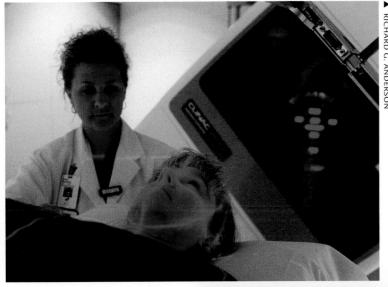

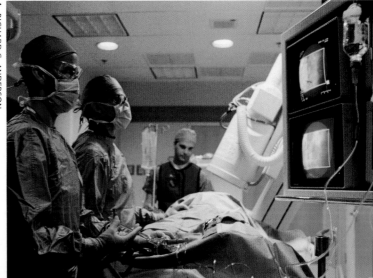

RICHARD G. ANDERSON

The 117-bed facility includes five critical care units, cardiovascular laboratories, dedicated heart surgery operating rooms, and a cardiac rehabilitation area, as well as clinical research facilities.

The physical design of many United facilities reflects the importance the hospital places on the mind/body connection. For instance, the John Nasseff Heart Hospital concentrates all levels of cardiac expertise within a single area, saving patients and their families confusion, extra steps, and often, extremely valuable minutes. The same is true in the hospital's Breast Center, where services are consolidated in one cozy, intimate environment to make a woman's experience as stress-free as possible.

The Breast Center offers a continuum of breast care services focusing on awareness and screening, diagnostic procedures, and, if necessary, breast surgery. The center brings professionals together, including members of the hospital's oncology staff, who guide women through their treatment options. It also offers personalized and sensitive care, including education, support groups, and the Appearance Center to help women who have concerns about their appearance during and after treatment.

The Oncology Department at United is also well known for its excellent comprehensive care programs for cancer patients. Staffed with dedicated cancer specialists, the department includes extensive subspecialty services and a highly trained nursing staff. In the Radiation Therapy Center, nationally

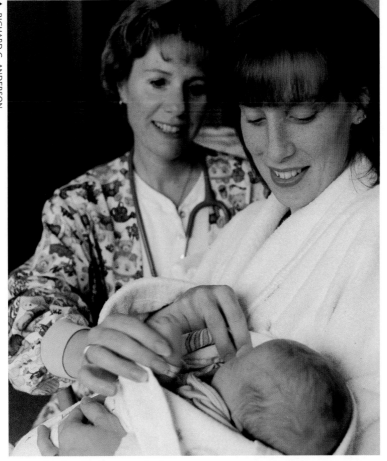

RICHARD G. ANDERSON

recognized radiation oncologists use state-of-the-art 3-D technology to allow more precise treatment planning and radiation therapy for all types of tumors. Specialty programs in oncology include high-dose chemotherapy with peripheral stem cell rescue, prostate seed implant therapy, and comprehensive surgical and medical treatment for central nervous system tumors.

The compassionate care and attention given each patient and his or her loved ones at United carries beyond these specialized areas to every unit—from the emergency

room to the operating rooms to the hospital's comprehensive rehabilitation services.

United Hospital's goal is to provide excellent and consistent service; learn constantly and anticipate tomorrow's needs; embrace differing points of view; use its resources wisely and retain the community's trust; and continue to build on its reputation of reliability, excellence, warmth, and compassion. As the hospital's mission statement states: "We provide an excellent health care experience for our patients and families."

THE HOSPITAL IS HIGHLY REGARDED FOR ITS EXCELLENT CLINICAL CARE, IN PART BECAUSE ITS STATE-OF-THE-ART TECHNOLOGY AND MODERN FACILITIES ATTRACT SOME OF THE MOST RENOWNED AND INNOVATIVE PRACTITIONERS IN THE COUNTRY (TOP LEFT AND RIGHT).

THE BIRTH CENTER OFFERS A COMPLETE RANGE OF MATERNITY SERVICES TO WOMEN WITH UNCOMPLICATED PREGNANCIES, AS WELL AS TO THOSE WITH HIGH-RISK PREGNANCIES (BOTTOM).

CBR Incorporated

CBR INCORPORATED IS A CLASSIC STORY OF HOW THE ENTREPRENEURIAL spirit—mixed with opportunity, creativity, determination, and lots of hard work—can become a winning combination. From its start as a single storefront on St. Paul's Grand Avenue, CBR has grown to become one of the key players in airport retailing across the country.

Founder and owner Carole Howe came to the attention of the Metropolitan Airports Commission (MAC) in 1974. MAC was looking for a minority business to fill a small retail space with something unique. Howe's Leather Indian store, then on Grand Avenue, fit the bill, and Howe decided to take up the challenge. TOUCH THE EARTH opened in January 1975 at the Minneapolis-

CBR INCORPORATED, WHICH WAS FOUNDED BY CAROLE HOWE, ATTRIBUTES ITS LEADERSHIP IN THE AIRPORT RETAIL INDUSTRY TO ITS TEAM OF COMMITTED PROFESSIONALS, CREATIVITY, AND HARD WORK (TOP).

"SNOOPY THE FLYING ACE"—SPONSORED BY CBR INCORPORATED—BROUGHT THE 50TH ANNIVERSARY CELEBRATION OF THE CARTOON'S CREATION TO THE MINNEAPOLIS ST. PAUL INTERNATIONAL AIRPORT (BOTTOM).

St. Paul International Airport, the first Native American airport store in the country.

Now, with 24 award-winning stores in eight major airports across the country, CBR Incorporated is a leader in airport retail. Howe praises MAC for its longstanding support: "They gave me my first opportunity, and along the way, the staff has been incredibly helpful. The partnership has meant that both the airport and CBR have flourished."

A Passion for Retail

From its beginning, one thing has remained constant at CBR Incorporated. The company's team is passionate about what they do: airport retail. "Carole has identified and hired professionals who are committed, creative, talented, and understand and love retail," says

Jim Stelten, CBR's chief operating officer.

Headquartered in St. Paul, CBR owns and operates four specialty retail concepts: SPIRIT OF THE RED HORSE features Native American/Western jewelry, lifestyle gifts, clothing, and home furnishings; BOW WOW MEOW offers gifts and treats for dog and cat owners and their favorite felines and canines; MINNESOTA! celebrates the state's regional delights; and CREATIVE KIDSTUFF—a Twin Cities-based, "Best of the Best" children's toy store—sells imaginative, non-violent toys, musical instruments and recordings, and other playthings.

This diversity of themes is grounded in a simple philosophy: "Love your customers and they will love you back," David Barthold, CBR's executive vice president says. "We work hard to make our customers feel welcome, special, and respected in our environments. It's the people—both the customers who visit and the employees who work here—who are the focus of our company's attention."

Outstanding in the Business

CBR Incorporated's success has been acknowledged by *Airport Retail News*, an industry publication in which airport professionals recently recognized the company with awards for "Best Airport Retailer," "Retailer with the Highest Regard for Customer Service," and "Best Store Design." CBR has been named one of the top 25 women-owned businesses in Minnesota for seven years running.

Reaching these peaks of accomplishment has come through planned growth. CBR's 24 stores are located in the Atlanta, Chicago, Los Angeles, Minneapolis-St. Paul, Orlando, Pittsburgh, and Portland, Oregon airports. The company's joint venture with The Paradies Shops has commitments for 15

additional stores at Minneapolis-St. Paul International Airport on the C and D Concourses, as well as in the Hubert H. Humphrey Terminal.

As an entrepreneur, Howe has been unafraid of change; in fact, she embraces it. Her TOUCH THE EARTH store has been reinvented as SPIRIT OF THE RED HORSE, redesigned from the ground up to capitalize on the strengths of the first venture, while incorporating new ideas and fresh design. SPIRIT OF THE RED HORSE, with 12 stores, is now the largest Native American/Western airport retail group in the country.

In May 1994, CBR opened an entirely new concept store, BOW WOW MEOW, at the then new Mall of America. This concept—now six stores strong—grew out of Howe's observation that her coworkers often thought of their pets as family. In the same year, the company opened its first regional store, MINNESOTA!, at the Minneapolis-St. Paul International Airport. At the airport's request, CBR has expanded to three MINNESOTA! store locations. Not the usual souvenir shop, MINNESOTA! features books, food, collectibles, clothing, and home decorating items themed to the state. Responding to the incredible success of the MINNESOTA! stores, CBR is currently developing regional concepts for airports across the country.

One key to CBR's success is Howe's belief in partnering, a philosophy of cooperation and partnership that pervades CBR and Howe's business strategy. "It's not just about money or success," she says. "It's about relationships and the bigger picture. It's about everyone doing well." Howe's newest store, CREATIVE KIDSTUFF, is a prime example. Howe collaborated with CREATIVE KIDSTUFF owner Cynthia Gerdes to bring the award-winning toy store to airport travelers. The first of these stores opened in October 2000 at the Pittsburgh International Airport, and is already the talk of the industry.

The CBR family has grown to 185 employees, and still maintains an environment that values the contributions of its people and nurtures their development. Howe says, "We joyfully celebrate the obligation of success that requires giving back." SPIRIT OF THE RED HORSE stores commit charitable dollars to programs that foster Native American education and artistic growth. First People's Fund, Museum of the American Indian (National Chapter), and Eagle's Nest women's shelter are among the company's affiliations. CBR's BOW WOW MEOW stores support local humane societies. The MINNESOTA! stores promote stewardship of the environment through programs such as Minnesota Boundary Waters camp scholarships.

With determination, professionalism, and a love of retail, CBR Incorporated has carved out a niche in the industry that continues to influence airport shopping nationwide.

CBR Incorporated, headquartered in St. Paul, owns and operates four retail concepts: SPIRIT OF THE RED HORSE, MINNESOTA!, BOW WOW MEOW, and CREATIVE KIDSTUFF.

F OR BUSINESSES WITH A COMPLEX ARRAY OF ORGANIZATIONAL NEEDS, Lawson Software offers the cutting-edge business enterprise software and Web-based technology to deal with everything from managing human resources to analyzing sales patterns. In the rapidly evolving e-business marketplace, Lawson pioneers the latest technology for

business management solutions.

"Lawson's corporate goal continues to be to leverage core competencies and advanced technology innovation, while extending the company's reach deep into the emerging markets of the digital economy," says Jay Coughlin, president and chief operating officer.

Founded in 1975, Lawson delivers leading-edge business management solutions that offer performance, reliability, and cost-effectiveness. The company serves numerous Fortune 2000 businesses, specializing in the financial services, health care, professional services, public sector, retail, and telecommunications industries. Lawson's list of customers includes such diverse organizations as Hard Rock Café, Allina Health System, and American

Floral Services Inc. The company is headquartered in St. Paul and London with additional offices throughout the United States and Europe.

THE TECHNOLOGY

E arly in the new millennium, Lawson debuted the next generation of its lawson.insight™ e-business product line. The lawson.insight product is designed to help companies gain competitive advantage by improving their financial, human resources, distribution, procurement, and analytic processes.

The latest generation of lawson.insight reflects Lawson's new strategic focus-building on the success of its traditional solutions with the latest mode of delivery through application service provider (ASP) channels. By accessing

the ASP delivery model, Lawson's e-business solutions can be generically resold and reused as extensions of Lawson's customers' businesses under their own brands. This strategy enlarges Lawson's revenue model and product extension capabilities.

"Today's market leaders are those providing the backbone—the infrastructure—for the emerging digital economy, and Lawson's new solution additions and strategic direction position it to become the leading provider of enterprise software powering e-business," Coughlin says. "In the electronic marketplace, your business can't wait. Companies have to leverage world-class technology and e-business automation to gain a competitive advantage now. Lawson can deliver that advantage today, as the e-business solutions powering the enterprise or digital community."

Part of what makes Lawson solutions so appealing to its customers is the Self-Evident Applications™ (SEA) product for e-business, which is unique to Lawson. This revolutionary software model uses point-and-click technologies introduced by the Internet to make software applications easily accessible to many people in a customer's organization.

For instance, conventional software applications for business management are based on forms or the type of transaction being performed. SEAs are information based. This means that the Web pages that appear prompt self-evident actions by the user. A company using this type of software would not need to go through the expensive and time-consuming employee training that is often needed when a new software application is installed.

Taking the holistic approach to a business's operations, Lawson can link and synchronize disparate systems to provide data that has never before been available.

"COMPANIES HAVE TO LEVERAGE WORLD-CLASS TECHNOLOGY AND E-BUSINESS AUTOMATION TO GAIN A COMPETITIVE ADVANTAGE NOW. LAWSON DELIVERS THAT ADVANTAGE TODAY," ACCORDING TO LAWSON SOFTWARE PRESIDENT AND COO JAY COUGHLIN.

LAWSON.COMMONS, LOCATED AT 380 ST. PETER STREET IN ST. PAUL, IS THE WORLDWIDE HEADQUARTERS FOR LAWSON SOFTWARE.

Combined with the real-time information that the latest technology can provide, this offers companies a powerful competitive tool.

"With more than 550 company-owned and franchise locations nationwide, we needed to understand our financial performance—days, nights, or weekends," says Lauren Cooper, vice president and controller for Outback Steakhouse. "By selecting Lawson's analytic capabilities, we will be able to view this critical information via a Web-based browser."

Lawson is recognized as the retail industry's preferred provider of e-business enterprise applications. Twenty-three of the top 100 North American restaurant chains and 19 of the top 100 North American retailers are part of Lawson's customer roster.

"Lawson has given us a competitive advantage," says Terry Byers, senior vice president and chief technology officer of American

Floral Services Inc. "For example, we have cut our order-to-shipment cycle from 30 days to just 24 hours in some cases. Another advantage is that every one of our business units has fingertip access to information that was unavailable before. We've cut our budget cycle in half and have reduced the time to close our monthly financials by at least 30 percent."

To stay at the forefront, Lawson uses its own innovative Evolving Practices™ research methodology in which business leaders are regularly surveyed to identify new information processing needs within different functions of their particular business. Lawson then incorporates these insights into its products to better serve its customers.

THE FUTURE

Lawson was the first organization to deploy business enterprise applications on the Web, as well as the first company to offer

self-evident Web interfaces, making the applications easily accessible and understandable. Now Lawson is again the pioneer by offering what the firm calls e-services. E-services are defined as business solutions or services provided interactively or automatically via a Web browser or a virtual provider network.

Just as with the newest generation of lawson.insight, the hardware, software, and even network needs for other Lawson products can now be hosted externally by an ASP. Lawson is working with several of its customers to show how this latest technology can be of benefit.

"These customers are forerunners in setting the tone for how businesses will buy enterprise applications and how the basic IT infrastructure will be delivered over time," says Coughlin. "Our goal at Lawson is not only to be on the frontier of the emerging digital market, but to dominate its role in our target markets."

ESTABLISHED IN ST. PAUL IN 1977, METRO COMMUTER SERVICES provides the citizens of the Twin Cities area with convenient, cost-effective transportation alternatives to driving to and from work alone. The agency is part of the state's Metropolitan Council, which oversees regional development and transportation services in the seven county Twin Cities area. Its services are free to businesses of all sizes to help promote options like car or van pooling, taking a bus, riding a bike, or even walking to work.

A BUSINESS PARTNERSHIP

Metro Commuter Services receives many requests from businesses for help in alerting employees to the advantages of alternative modes of transportation and to money-saving programs, says Patty Carlson, manager for Metro Commuter Services.

Often, a business will contact Metro Commuter Services when relocating. Since every employee will need to change his or her route to work, having information on transportation alternatives will help make the transition easier, Carlson says.

As a first step in creating awareness of its mission, Metro Commuter Services may help organize and provide promotional materials at a commuter fair or brown-bag lunch on-site at a company. Employees can pick up information about various transportation options, and a transit representative will give them route and schedule specifics.

A database maintained by Metro Commuter Services contains information on people throughout the region interested in sharing a ride to work, so employees can locate someone who lives and works near them. Currently, there are approximately 35,000 names in the database, which is updated yearly, Carlson says. In 1999 alone, approximately 15,000 new people were added.

For those who may hesitate to carpool or take the bus for fear they will not have a way home if there is an emergency, Metro Commuter Services offers a program called Guaranteed Ride Home. Anyone who takes a bus, van- or carpools, rides a bike, or walks to work at

least three days a week is eligible to receive two coupons good for a free cab ride home. There is no cost to be part of the program.

"It's like an insurance policy," Carlson says, adding that there are 21,000 people currently in the Guaranteed Ride Home program and that the redemption rate of the coupons is less than 7 percent.

Research has shown that employees who take the bus or carpool to work—besides reducing air pollution and road congestion—are more likely to arrive on time, be less stressed when they arrive, and stay for a full day of work.

PAID TO SEEK ALTERNATIVES

Economics also provide an incentive for employees to seek transportation alternatives. For those who van- or carpool with five or more people, Metro Commuter Services will give the driver $50 a month for the first five months to help establish the pool. "That money can go for parking or gas, or even to buy doughnuts or pizza," Carlson says, adding that someone simply has to register the super pool with Metro Commuter Services. "It helps them get started," she says.

METRO COMMUTER SERVICES PROVIDES THE CITIZENS OF THE TWIN CITIES AREA WITH CONVENIENT, COST-EFFECTIVE TRANSPORTATION ALTERNATIVES TO DRIVING TO AND FROM WORK ALONE.

Currently, there are 5,500 registered car and van pools in the Twin Cities, but Carlson believes there are many more that have not formally registered. "The number of pools has increased every year," Carlson says. Other advantages of riding together include use of less congested, high-occupancy-vehicle lanes; specially reserved free parking spots for van and car pools in downtown St. Paul; the shared cost of gas; and the friendships that can develop in the ride-share situation.

Another clear-cut advantage to seeking transportation alternatives is the Commuter Check program,

a voucher for bus fare or van pool costs that companies can offer employees as a tax-free benefit—either a supplemental benefit or a pretax salary deduction up to $65 each month. Employers save on FICA, disability, unemployment, workmen's compensation, and other payroll-linked costs. Typically, employees get 40 percent more in after-tax value, while employers save 10 percent in payroll-related costs.

"A lot of employers are not aware of what we offer," Carlson says. "It's a way to do something nice for your employee."

For hardy souls, riding a bike to

work is a popular alternative—even in the Minnesota winter. Bike lockers provided by Metro Commuter Services are available in downtown St. Paul year-round, Carlson says.

To underscore the increasing popularity of alternative modes of transportation, the new RiverCenter parking ramp will include 100 bike lockers and 200 reserved spaces for car and van pools to meet the increased demand.

"Some employers use us because they feel it's the right thing to do for the community," says Carlson. "What gets most people to do it is the time and the money they can save."

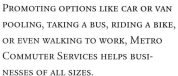

PROMOTING OPTIONS LIKE CAR OR VAN POOLING, TAKING A BUS, RIDING A BIKE, OR EVEN WALKING TO WORK, METRO COMMUTER SERVICES HELPS BUSINESSES OF ALL SIZES.

RESEARCH HAS SHOWN THAT EMPLOYEES WHO TAKE THE BUS OR CARPOOL TO WORK ARE MORE LIKELY TO ARRIVE ON TIME, BE LESS STRESSED WHEN THEY ARRIVE, AND STAY FOR A FULL DAY OF WORK.

FLANNERY CONSTRUCTION

L IKE OTHER SUCCESSFUL CONSTRUCTION COMPANIES, FLANNERY Construction owes its continued success to quality work, but what makes the company special is its heart. ▣ Gerry Flannery, CEO, is as proud of his employees and the company's social conscience as he is of the quality construction the company has done since the 1970s. When asked

about the company's formula for success, Flannery credits the employees who have been with him for decades—the craftspeople who work so hard in the field and the office staff who make sure everything flows harmoniously.

With this kind of attitude, it is not surprising that Flannery Construction belongs to St. Paul, a city dedicated to its community neighborhoods and renowned for its quality of life.

PROMISING GROWTH

F lannery Construction began when Flannery and a fellow carpenter began remodeling the old Victorian homes that line the Ramsey Hill neighborhood. The groundwork for success was laid with every piece of millwork, kitchen and bathroom remodel, and small construction job. Slowly, surely, the company expanded.

Currently, the company employs 45 people in the field and a staff of six in its downtown St. Paul office. In addition, more than

FLANNERY CONSTRUCTION'S PROJECT WITH INDIANHEAD SCOUTING—THE BOY SCOUTS OF AMERICA'S ST. PAUL HEADQUARTERS—FEATURES A ROTUNDA CEILING.

THE EMPLOYEES OF FLANNERY CON-STRUCTION ARE THE HEART OF THE COMPANY'S SUCCESS.

a quarter of the employees are women and minorities. Supervisor Mark Welch, who has been with the company for 17 years, says, "I've always been proud of helping break down those barriers in construction."

The company performs a wide range of commercial and residential construction jobs throughout the Twin Cities metropolitan area, including work for several nonprofit organizations.

"Nonprofit organizations are working with limited resources and big dreams," Flannery says. His job is to fit the budget to the dreams, and his tailoring seems to be working, as satisfied clients refer others and return themselves for future work. The company stands by its mission of providing fine quality craftsmanship at an affordable price, within budget and on time.

Flannery Construction recently created a multiuse development called the Brownstone Project on University Avenue for Model Cities of St. Paul. The company "just has a feel for groups like us," says Beverley Hawkins, Model Cities of St. Paul CEO. "We're an organization that doesn't have a lot of money, but Flannery always figures out a way to make things work."

RETAINING QUALITY PEOPLE

D edication to making things work is perhaps one of the reasons employees seem to stay with Flannery, who is proud to point out that many of his staff have been with him since the beginning.

"People tend to stick around," says Flannery. "We treat people fairly, and we try to keep the tone positive—both in the office and in

◀ YALE GREENFIELD

the field." Flannery supports employee education and training, as well as health club membership. He also contributes his barbecue talents and unique recipes as chef at the company's quarterly meetings.

"The way Flannery treats you, you want to do more," says 10-year employee Bob Vassar, a materials handler. "I like working for the company. It's kind of like a family where everybody means something to the company."

Marsha Hartman, who has managed Flannery's office for more than a decade, says, "I know that this company will behave in ways that match my moral values. There are altruistic things that happen here in the workplace. We have a commitment to helping

nonprofits. We're in business to make money, and we've been successful. But we are on the same side as the client."

BUSINESS FOCUS

Flannery, who traded his carpenter's belt for a computer in 1984, is a frequent visitor to his construction sites. He evaluates and assesses the feasibility of projects before construction documents are drawn up, and he continues to help through all stages of a project's development. "That's how we build a relationship with a client," Flannery says.

That's why Flannery's jobs include restaurants like Sakura and Da Vinci in St. Paul and BRAVO! Meeting and Event Center in Min-

neapolis; elaborate millwork and fine finish work that grace the Minnesota Judicial Center and the Tea House at the Como Ordway Memorial Japanese Garden; tenant remodeling, such as the 160,000-square-foot St. Paul office of the Army Corps of Engineers and multiple sites of the Minneapolis YWCA; community health clinics and day care remodeling throughout the metro area; and housing ranging from quality affordable housing to historic renovation to unique private designs requiring extra attention to detail.

Flannery feels a responsibility not only to clients, but to the industry as well. He is committed to helping young people in the trades, and participates in various internship programs. And all of Flannery's hard work pays off: His employees are loyal, his customers come back, and the company's dedication to community was rewarded in 1997 when Flannery was nominated for the Chamber of Commerce-sponsored Walter and Lydia Deubener Award for Small Business Innovation. Flannery Construction has also been acknowledged by both cities—St. Paul and Minneapolis—for its successes in meeting and exceeding affirmative action goals.

Consistently on time and on budget, quality jobs with a heart characterize Flannery Construction, and will position the company for continuing success in St. Paul and beyond.

CLOCKWISE FROM TOP LEFT: MINNEAPOLIS' BRAVO! MEETING AND EVENT CENTER, BUILT BY FLANNERY CONSTRUCTION, COMBINES FINE DINING WITH A LIVELY DOWNTOWN FEELING.

FLANNERY'S FINE FINISH WORK CREATES A WARM AMBIENCE FOR ST. PAUL'S SAKURA RESTAURANT.

THE INTERIOR OF THE TEA HOUSE AT ST. PAUL'S COMO ORDWAY MEMORIAL JAPANESE GARDEN BLENDS GENTLY INTO THE NATURAL SURROUNDINGS.

MODEL CITIES OF ST. PAUL CEO BEVERLEY HAWKINS SHARES A LAUGH AT THE BROWNSTONE PROJECT WITH FLANNERY CONSTRUCTION FOREMAN KENNETH ALLEN (LEFT) AND COMPANY OWNER GERRY FLANNERY.

OR THREE DECADES, METROPOLITAN STATE UNIVERSITY—METRO STATE— has been filling a unique educational niche in the Twin Cities. With nearly 8,000 students ranging from 16 to 75 years old, the university is renowned. ◼ "The professors know students are probably juggling jobs and families, so they're more flexible," explains Pam McCurdy Ellington,

director of communications and marketing for the university. Noting that Metro State will accommodate students transferring credits from other colleges or universities, Ellington says the operative words are "we want to work with you."

Metro State's degree programs address the needs of today's marketplace, so those students returning to college can refresh their knowledge base and be assured that they have the most up-to-date skills available, Ellington says. "We're serving the future of the Twin Cities," she says, adding that graduates work at some of the most prestigious companies in the city.

Students may chose from 40 undergraduate and graduate programs, including traditional bachelor's degrees as well as undergraduate degrees in social work and nursing. Graduate

programs at Metro State include Master of Business Administration, Master of Science in Nursing, Master of Management Information Systems, and Master of Science in Technical Communication.

RECOGNIZED FOR EXCELLENCE

The university, which is one of Minnesota's seven state universities, has been recognized nationally for excellence in teaching, and prides itself on its small class sizes and the innovative programs offered. For example, the new urban teacher education program focuses the student teaching experience on core urban schools, so students learn firsthand how to work with a diverse student body effectively. The groundbreaking program is intended to increase the number of minority teachers and attract low-income, first-generation college students to teaching careers, Ellington says.

The accounting program at Metro State also is nationally recognized for the number of alumni passing the Certified Management Accountant (CMA) exam. In Minnesota, Metro State graduates consistently score at the top on the Minnesota Certified Public Accountant (CPA) exam. The program is so well regarded, in fact, that the

Minnesota CPA Society selected Metro State over larger area business schools in the Twin Cities to oversee the society's continuing education programs.

As Metro State serves its students, so it also serves the community through its Center for Community-Based Learning. Every year, the campus is opened to the adjacent Dayton's Bluff neighborhood schoolchildren for the College for Kids. First through sixth graders "apply" to the university, and then spend a day learning about computers, doing experiments with the science faculty, and participating in other activities to acquaint them with college. The university also provides volunteer mentors for area high school students.

The proposed new library complex for the university will be built in partnership with the St. Paul Public Library and will be open to the larger community. This national model not only will serve university students and the neighborhood, but also will narrow the digital divide by offering Internet access to those without computers.

"If you talk to the students here, a lot of them will say if it wasn't for Metro State, they wouldn't be going to college," Ellington says. "We're giving the business community a more educated populace."

WITH NEARLY 8,000 STUDENTS RANGING IN AGE FROM 16 TO 75 YEARS OLD, METROPOLITAN STATE UNIVERSITY IS RENOWNED FOR TAILORING THE ACADEMIC PROGRAM TO FIT THE INDIVIDUAL STUDENT'S NEEDS.

SAINT PAUL

1980-2001

SCHREIBER MULLANEY CONSTRUCTION CO., INC.

SCHREIBER MULLANEY CONSTRUCTION CO., INC. IS ONE OF THE CITY'S fastest-growing companies, but the firm manages to maintain its small-business feel. Founding partners Bruce Schreiber and Tim Mullaney try always to remember that some of the smallest jobs they landed some 20 years ago ultimately became some of their company's largest projects.

"We've maintained that down-home sense," Schreiber says. "It's personal contact that got us to where we are."

One day recently, a local store found Schreiber Mullaney in the phone book and called to ask whether the company would fix a dressing room door. With $15 million in annual revenues, and a résumé of projects that include some of the hottest, upscale restaurants in the Twin Cities—as well as Burger King and Denny's, schools, churches, and work on Underwater World at the Mall of America—Schreiber Mullaney could easily have afforded to say no to this minor repair project. Instead, the company sent a carpenter out to do the job.

Over the years, there have been countless other instances of little jobs done well, which led to referrals for bigger jobs and important connections with prominent architectural firms and major businesses. Seventy percent of the firm's business is gained by referral.

SCHREIBER MULLANEY CONSTRUCTION CO., INC. FOSTERS SOLID RELATIONSHIPS WITH ITS VENDORS AND SUBCONTRACTORS, HAVING ESTABLISHED A REPUTATION FOR FOLLOWING THROUGH ON COMMITMENTS AND PROCESSING ACCOUNTS PAYABLE IN A TIMELY FASHION.

"These little crumbs have turned into bread," Schreiber says. The secret, he adds, lies in the company's quality work, as well as its honesty and integrity. "If we say we're going to do something, we do it," says Schreiber. "If you treat people right, good things come from it."

HANGING THE BAGS

Back in 1981, Schreiber and Mullaney were just graduating from the carpentry program at St. Paul Technical College. The economy was in recession and there were minimal opportunities for the two friends, who wanted to start their own construction business.

"We started with very small jobs—storm windows, cabinets, stuff for relatives and friends, whatever we could get," Schreiber says. "We've had to work very hard to build this business and it hasn't always been easy."

Schreiber and Mullaney's big break came when they received a contract to remodel a Walgreens drugstore. Their work was so impressive that the Walgreens chain asked them to work on an additional 15 locations in the Twin Cities. By the mid-1980s, Schreiber Mullaney's revenue averaged between $1 million and $1.5 million per year.

Because they also worked as subcontractors—hanging the tool

bags, as they say in the business—Schreiber and Mullaney learned how they wanted to manage their business, in their relationships both with their clients and with their own personnel.

"We're carpenters," Schreiber says. "We know the industry. We don't have people do things we know are unrealistic." The company retains some of the best carpenters in the area, and prides itself on the state-of-the-art equipment it provides its workers, the cleanliness of its job sites, and its efficiency and good communication with everyone involved in each project.

Schreiber Mullaney also fosters solid relationships with its vendors and subcontractors, having established a reputation for following through on commitments and processing accounts payable in a timely fashion.

"Our suppliers and subcontractors are real assets to us," Schreiber says. "By taking care of them, we ensure that they'll take care of us."

As the word spread about the quality of Schreiber and Mullaney's work, and about their honesty and integrity, they found that they needed to formalize their business.

In 1995, the two bought and renovated a building in St. Paul, and then hired an office manager. One year later, they hired their first project manager. Today, Schreiber Mullaney has a payroll of about 20 employees.

The booming economy brought astronomical growth to Schreiber Mullaney. Between 1994 and 1996, the company saw 121 percent growth. *CityBusiness*, the local weekly business journal, found Schreiber Mullaney to be one of the fastest-growing companies in the Twin Cities in the late 1990s.

STRATEGY FOR THE FUTURE

Schreiber and Mullaney would like to maintain their business at the current level, and they have no plans for expansion. "We're comfortable here," Schreiber says. "It works out well. We can logistically take care of our clients."

At this point, with the prospect of an inevitable downturn in the economy, Schreiber Mullaney is beginning to increase the company's name recognition through marketing. Because the company's client list is so diverse, Schreiber is not

concerned that a shift in the economy will greatly affect the business.

"In 1987, we were nearly bankrupt because we had put all our eggs in one basket, so to speak," Schreiber says. "When it went bad, it really went bad. We learned a lesson from that, and it is why we're so diversified now."

Besides high-end restaurants like Oceanaire Seafood Room, Chino Latino, Tejas, Basil's Restaurant, and the New French Cafe, Schreiber Mullaney has also constructed 14 spaces in the food court at the Mall of America, as well as many Burger King and Denny's restaurants throughout the Twin Cities. The company has completed dozens of remodeling and construction jobs for St. Paul Public Schools, in addition to a wide variety of retail and office projects. While Schreiber Mullaney no longer does any residential construction, the company continues to receive calls requesting services for residential projects.

"We've really developed our own heritage," Schreiber says. "We're a first-generation company at a second-generation level right now. And it has all depended on the relationships we've built."

SCHREIBER MULLANEY IS ONE OF THE CITY'S FASTEST-GROWING COMPANIES, BUT THE FIRM MANAGES TO MAINTAIN ITS SMALL-BUSINESS FEEL.

E MBASSY SUITES SAINT PAUL'S ATTENTION TO DETAIL IS EVIDENT FROM THE moment guests step off the plane at the Minneapolis-St. Paul International Airport. A quick call to the hotel summons a van stocked with beverages and newspapers to whisk guests to the Embassy Suites. The driver can give passengers a rundown of the hotel's other services,

as well as information on local attractions, on the 15-minute ride. In addition, guests can go through the express check-in procedure en route, so there is no need to wait at the front desk to check in.

Upon arriving at the elegant brick hotel in downtown St. Paul, visitors are enveloped by the lush atmosphere and sunny warmth of the structure's central, eight-story atrium filled with more than 7,000 plants and trees. The soothing sound of water running over rocks and into a pond—stocked with several South American ring-necked teal—can be heard throughout the towering atrium.

"The whole atmosphere of the hotel is to feel like a welcome home," says Julie Larson, director of sales and marketing. "We strive to create a warm, inviting feeling."

ACCOMMODATIONS AND SERVICES

O nce visitors arrive, they can go directly to their suite, bypassing the front-desk check-in and proceeding straight to work or rest. The standard accommoda-

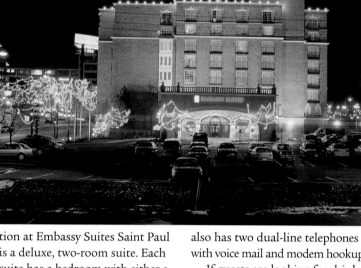

tion at Embassy Suites Saint Paul is a deluxe, two-room suite. Each suite has a bedroom with either a king-size bed or two double beds, remote control television with cable and the latest movies on demand, telephone, and bathroom with full amenities, including hair dryer. The living room has a sofa bed, armchair, television, wet bar, refrigerator, microwave, coffeemaker, and well-lit dining table with space to spread out and work or study. Each suite

also has two dual-line telephones with voice mail and modem hookup.

If guests are looking for drinks and microwavable food to fill the suite's refrigerator, the gift shop in the lobby area stocks a variety of items. Other hotel amenities include a swimming pool, whirlpool, sauna and steam room with towels provided, and fitness room. To help businesspeople look their best, a dry-cleaning service is available during the week, and there are washers and dryers on two of the floors, as well as a full-size iron and ironing board in each suite. To keep visitors informed about all the news that affects them, *USA Today* is delivered Monday through Friday to the door of each suite.

AMENITIES AND FEATURES

G uests at Embassy Suites Saint Paul can also take advantage of the daily meal and social gatherings the hotel sponsors. The all-inclusive plan offers a complimentary, cooked-to-order breakfast every morning, as well as a complimentary, two-hour Manager's Reception each evening, featuring top-shelf liquors and soft drinks of choice.

Breakfast and the nightly Manager's Reception also are times for guests to mingle in an informal and relaxed environment away

from work. "It's very easy to bond with a coworker at breakfast or at the cocktail reception," Julie Larson says. "The atmosphere promotes camaraderie, which is something corporate meeting planners appreciate, given the fact that they are bringing in employees from all over the United States and in some cases, the world. It's easy, instant networking. A full-service restaurant and an Irish pub/sports bar with a big-screen television and access to any sporting event are right on the premises."

"It's another way for people to get together," says Rosco Larson, general manager. "People from New York and Los Angeles can watch their home teams. Single travelers can get a bite to eat and watch sports, news, or local channels without feeling out of place."

If visitors want to venture out to other parts of the city, the hotel can accommodate. For a small fee, the night life shuttle service will take guests to the lively shops and restaurants of Grand Avenue in St. Paul, as well as to the Mall of America, downtown Minneapolis, or other area attractions.

WELCOMING BUSINESS TRAVELERS

While it welcomes all guests regardless of the reason for their visits, Embassy Suites Saint Paul strives to be the hotel of choice for business travelers. For many Embassy Suites guests, this will indeed be their home away from home as they interview for a job, take special training, consult at a

local corporation, or relocate, along with their families, to St. Paul for a new job. Companies headquartered in St. Paul—which include 3M, Minnesota Life, Ecolab, Lawson Software, and the St. Paul Companies—regularly make arrangements for job candidates and employees

from other locations in the United States and abroad to stay at the Embassy Suites Saint Paul.

"These companies expect the hotel they choose to give a fair representation of their company, as to quality and level of service," says Julie Larson. "The Embassy Suites Saint Paul strives and succeeds to be a true reflection of the quality and style of the company."

The hotel can accommodate any length of stay, from a few days to longer than a week, and the staff works diligently to make sure guests' needs are met. "We've got a lot of loyalty here among the staff," Rosco Larson says. "Our management team has 150 years of experience between us, and we're fairly young."

As Rosco Larson says, "Individuals are very happy with their company when they're allowed to stay here. They appreciate the suite upgrade and the idea that their company has chosen such deluxe accommodations for them."

THE STANDARD ACCOMMODATION AT EMBASSY SUITES SAINT PAUL IS A DELUXE, TWO-ROOM SUITE, WITH EITHER A KING-SIZE BED OR TWO DOUBLE BEDS, A REMOTE CONTROL TELEVISION WITH CABLE, A TELEPHONE, AND MANY ADDITIONAL AMENITIES TO MAKE GUESTS FEEL AT EASE.

WHILE IT WELCOMES ALL GUESTS REGARDLESS OF THE REASON FOR THEIR VISITS, EMBASSY SUITES SAINT PAUL STRIVES TO BE THE HOTEL OF CHOICE FOR BUSINESS TRAVELERS.

SUN COUNTRY AIRLINES HAS BEEN A MEMBER OF THE TWIN CITIES MARKET-place since 1983, when it began as a charter airline. Offering the community an alternative in air travel, the airline has become known for its competitive fares and its sunny disposition. In 1999, Sun Country began scheduled service and began competing head-on with the other major

airline in the market.

Citing U.S. Department of Transportation figures, Tammy Lee, vice president, corporate affairs, says that since Sun Country entered the market with scheduled service, the airline has saved the flying public $120 million a year. "The public was crying out for competition," Lee says, adding that the company's slogan, We're Here For You, is not just a marketing motto, but reflects how the company sees itself in the community.

A DIFFERENT KIND OF AIRLINE

Lower fares are what attracted many people to the upstart airline at the beginning. But as its major competitor began matching those fares, Sun Country officials knew the airline's corporate philosophy would ultimately set Sun Country apart.

"We're not just another chair in the air," Lee says. "A lot of airlines believe their job is just to get people from point A to point B. We believe we're in the hospitality industry. We've raised the bar when it comes to service."

The key to Sun Country's success in the service area is its people. Marketing in the airline industry is generally focused on price, product, placement, and promotion. While each of those elements is essential to success, Sun Country believes people are just as important.

"Our employees are first," Lee says of the approximately 1,400 people who make up Sun Country. "If you truly do put the employee first, they will, in turn, put the customer first."

Stories abound of Sun Country flight attendants who identify with the airline's mission and put forth that extra effort to please passengers. For instance, when one passenger mentioned that he would love a latte, the flight attendant steamed some milk, whipped it to a froth as best she could with a fork, and delivered the milk and coffee to him, saying, "I did the best I could." "We don't take ourselves too seriously, but we take our mission very seriously," Lee says.

Employees are empowered to make decisions on the spot without referring to voluminous guideline books or calling on superiors, Lee

says. Sun Country leaves it up to the employee on the scene to decide the best way to compensate an inconvenienced passenger, based on the particular situation.

"We try to be very honest and forthright with the customer," Lee says. "We give out flight discounts or tickets that are appropriate for the inconvenience they've experienced."

Sun Country, which flies to several dozen destinations in the United States, the Caribbean, Mexico, and Central America, is based at the Hubert H. Humphrey (HHH) Terminal at the Minneapolis/St.

BILL LA MACCHIA JR. IS CURRENT PRESIDENT AND CEO OF SUN COUNTRY AIRLINES (TOP).

SUN COUNTRY AIRLINES, WHICH FLIES TO SEVERAL DOZEN DESTINATIONS IN THE UNITED STATES, THE CARIBBEAN, MEXICO, AND CENTRAL AMERICA, IS BASED AT HUBERT H. HUMPHREY (HHH) TERMINAL AT THE MINNEAPOLIS/ST. PAUL INTERNATIONAL AIRPORT (BOTTOM LEFT AND RIGHT).

Paul International Airport. This smaller terminal may lack some of the amenities of the larger main terminal, but Sun Country accommodates its customers with regular free shuttle service to the main terminal, as well as to the nearby Mall of America, if there is a delay in flights.

"We do our best with the resources available," Lee says, noting that parking is often easier at HHH, and passengers never have far to walk between the ticket counter and the boarding gate. In May 2001, Sun Country will become the anchor tenant in a new, state-of-the-art terminal, which will include more amenities. The airline is also anticipating delivery of eight new 737-800 airplanes complete with leather seating throughout, the most advanced technology on the flight deck, and dual class seating.

The friendly, fun attitude of many of Sun Country's employees filters down from President and CEO Bill La Macchia Jr. "When Bill flies, he really does help fold blankets and pick up meal trays," Lee says. The airline's advertising campaign encourages people in the community to feel that they have a relationship with La Macchia. Customers can even e-mail him directly from Sun Country's Web site.

SPECIAL BUSINESS FARES

To attract business travelers, Sun Country has developed a unique program called Onefare. Businesses large or small can use this free program in which any round-trip ticket costs $260, with no advance purchase or Saturday night stay required. In turn, the

business must commit to 20 round-trips in a 12-month period. "We've had independent consultants signing up together to hit the 20-trip mark," Lee says.

Studies have shown that 25 percent of business travelers take their families with them, so Sun Country has extended the Onefare program to include family members. For those larger corporations that have an in-house travel service or use a travel agency, Sun Country offers the Private Fare program, where the rate is negotiated depending on the volume of travel to which the business can commit.

Sun Country has also formed relationships in the community through its service projects, raising money for the Ronald McDonald House—where families with children battling cancer stay while undergoing treatment—and the Greater Minneapolis Crisis Nursery, among others.

"The community has responded—and responded warmly—and we're grateful," says Lee. "They say, 'It's great to have you in the market.' And we say, 'Fly us when you can—and tell a friend to fly us, too.' We make it easier and more affordable for everyone to fly."

THE KEY TO SUN COUNTRY'S SUCCESS IN THE SERVICE AREA IS ITS PEOPLE.

OFFERING THE TWIN CITIES MARKET AN ALTERNATIVE IN AIR TRAVEL SINCE 1983, SUN COUNTRY AIRLINES HAS BECOME KNOWN FOR ITS COMPETITIVE FARES AND ITS SUNNY DISPOSITION.

ORDWAY CENTER FOR THE PERFORMING ARTS

OFTEN CALLED THE JEWEL OF ST. PAUL, ORDWAY CENTER FOR THE Performing Arts is a destination that offers world-class performances in the heart of the Twin Cities. Serving more than 500,000 patrons a year, the size and scope of its presentations make Ordway Center unique to Minnesota. "We have always believed that Ordway Center

ORDWAY CENTER FOR THE PERFORMING ARTS—OFTEN CALLED THE JEWEL OF ST. PAUL—IS A DESTINATION THAT OFFERS WORLD-CLASS PERFORMANCES IN THE HEART OF THE TWIN CITIES (LEFT).

ORDWAY CENTER'S U.S. BANK THEATER SEASON FEATURES TOURING BROADWAY-STYLE SHOWS, SUCH AS *Rent*, AS WELL AS PRODUCTIONS THAT ARE CREATED FROM BEGINNING TO END BY THE CENTER (RIGHT).

for the Performing Arts is more than a magnificent building for live performances," says Ordway Center President and CEO Kevin McCollum. "We offer an arts experience that welcomes all audiences and consistently delivers the finest performing arts in the state."

Ordway Center for the Performing Arts includes two theaters—the 1,900-seat Main Hall and the 308-seat McKnight Theatre. From the St. Petersburg Ballet on Ice, which required the creation of an ice-skating rink, to classical music concerts, the theaters have accommodated a wide spectrum of the performing arts since opening on January 1, 1985.

SERVING THE COMMUNITY

Ordway Center for the Performing Arts is named for Lucius Pond Ordway, a prominent St. Paul businessman and early investor in 3M. Sally Ordway Irvine, Ordway's granddaughter, led the campaign to build a new theater in downtown St. Paul and chose the name.

Irvine, who died in 1987, had always loved the theater. She was dismayed when the St. Paul Civic Auditorium closed its doors in 1980, leaving no place to enjoy theater in downtown St. Paul. Irvine envisioned a venue for theater, music, opera, dance, and even the circus.

To make Irvine's vision a reality for the people of St. Paul, the Ordway family contributed $15 million to build Ordway Center for the Performing Arts. The balance of the $26 million needed to build the center came from foundations, corporations, and individuals in the largest private fund drive for an arts facility in Minnesota. The only public contribution was a small portion of the site conveyed by the City of St. Paul. To this day, Ordway Center for the Performing Arts is one of the few such centers in the country that does not receive ongoing city support.

The building that materialized from the generosity of the community is an architectural gem overlooking Rice Park in the heart of downtown St. Paul. The building's architect, Benjamin Thompson of Benjamin Thompson & Associates, Cambridge, Massachusetts, described it as "a theater where . . . harmonies are for both eye and ear, where sound and vision, color and light flow together in an artful unity of theater and life."

All three levels of the building's lobby overlook Rice Park. Cream-colored walls, Honduran mahogany woodwork, and tulip-shaped globes hanging in the three-story stairwell with its sweeping spiral staircase create a sense of drama, warmth, and glamour.

To achieve the highest acoustical standards, the Main Hall blends state-of-the-art engineering and classic craftsmanship. The traditional hard, sound-reflective surfaces of plaster and wood can be "tuned" for different uses through adjustable, sound-absorbing panels built into the walls and ceiling.

PHILLIP PROWSE

JOAN MARCUS

LIVE FROM ST. PAUL

Each year, Ordway Center for the Performing Arts presents as well as produces the U.S. Bank Theater Season, featuring a series of Broadway-style shows. Some of these productions are touring shows, such as *Rent* and *Les Misérables*, while the others are created from beginning to end by Ordway Center.

The planet Ordway® Target® Season consists of theater, music, dance, and puppetry performed by outstanding artists from around the world. This season was created to reflect and celebrate the region's growing cultural diversity. The programs for the planet Ordway Target Season are selected in consultation with cultural advisers who represent the Twin Cities' four largest ethnic communities: African-American, American Indian, Asian/Pacific, and Chicano/Latino. The season features local performing arts organizations, as well as groups from around the globe.

Starting in 2001, Ordway Center for the Performing Arts became the host of the Koch International Children's Festival. This annual festival is an opportunity for children from age four to fourth grade and their families to gather in St. Paul to celebrate the performing arts and youth. This is the first such festival to be offered in the Midwest and features some of the world's foremost performing arts events for young people. The Koch International is one of the largest international children's performing arts festivals in the nation.

For more than a decade, Ordway Center has been at the forefront of educational programming in the arts. The centerpiece of the program is called Performing Arts Classrooms, sponsored by 3M and serving some 35,000 students a year, most of them from the inner-city schools. Other education initiatives include Insights (preperformance lectures), master classes, Ordway Center Arts Dialogues, and classroom residencies in collaboration with area artists.

Ordway Center for the Performing Arts is home to four resident arts organizations: the Minnesota Opera, Schubert Club, Saint Paul Chamber Orchestra, and Minnesota Orchestra.

FRANZ HALL

STARS OF THE COMMUNITY

Ordway Center for the Performing Arts was built with the community in mind, and the community has continued to support it enthusiastically. The Ordway Circle of Stars™ is a nonprofit corporation of volunteers who educate the community and provide support for the Ordway Center through educational programs and fund-raising events.

Founded in 1995, the Ordway Circle of Stars boasts nearly 300 members. In just five years, its annual fund-raising total increased from $35,000 to $400,000, helping support programs like the Performing Arts Classroom, which provides inexpensive matinee tickets and free buses for schoolchildren.

Thanks to the initiative of Sally Ordway Irvine and the continuing support of hundreds of volunteers, Ordway Center for the Performing Arts has become the cultural centerpiece of downtown St. Paul.

SERVING MORE THAN 500,000 PATRONS A YEAR, THE SIZE AND SCOPE OF ITS PRESENTATIONS MAKE ORDWAY CENTER UNIQUE TO MINNESOTA.

ORDWAY CENTER FOR THE PERFORMING ARTS IS NAMED FOR LUCIUS POND ORDWAY, A PROMINENT ST. PAUL BUSINESSMAN AND EARLY INVESTOR IN 3M.

H ISTORICALLY, St. Paul is probably best known for shipping and manufacturing, railroads, and breweries. Yet during the last 50 years, the city's reputation as a place for great beer had begun to slip as several large breweries started closing. That decline was stopped in its tracks in 1986 with the founding of Summit Brewing Company.

Today, St. Paul is back on the brewing map again.

Summit was launched by Mark Stutrud, president and head brewer, with just $540,000 in financing and a handful of private investors. Stutrud began brewing in a converted automotive transmission shop on University Avenue in St. Paul. That first year, Stutrud and his four employees rolled out 1,500 barrels of Extra Pale Ale, much of which they delivered themselves in kegs to area bars. Still in its infancy, the brewery didn't have distributors or bottling capacity at that point.

THE REAL EVIDENCE OF SUMMIT'S SUCCESS IS IN THE BEER THE COMPANY PRODUCES. "PEOPLE TEND TO THINK THAT BEER IS JUST A BEVERAGE SIMILAR TO SODA. BUT IT'S REALLY MUCH MORE COMPLEX AND CHALLENGING," SAYS MARK STUTRUD, PRESIDENT AND HEAD BREWER.

NEW BUILDINGS, NEW BREWS

J ust a year later, however, the fledgling brewery had installed bottling equipment and had established relationships with wholesalers to distribute its products, which by then included a second ale, Great Northern Porter. Four years after its founding, Summit was turning a profit. In 1992, Stutrud leased an adjacent building, a move that allowed the brewery to meet the growing demand for its beer.

The company's growth was so phenomenal that by the mid-1990s, Stutrud knew he would have to find a new home for Summit. In 1996, he purchased the firm's current site from the city's Port Authority. The new brewery is located in Crosby Lake Business Park, "a very progressive development by the Port Authority of St. Paul to reutilize urban land, return the property to the tax rolls, and create good jobs," Stutrud explains.

"This is the first brewery to be designed and built from the ground up in St. Paul in 100 years," says Stutrud. "We started very small in the Midway area of St. Paul more than 14 years ago, and have grown to have a sizable market presence."

The new Summit brewery was designed by local architect Peter O'Brien. With large windows overlooking the wooded banks of the river, the brewery melds a contemporary feel with a sense of tradition, including warm wood details and the rich copper of the huge, prominently displayed brewing kettles. "The building embellishes and illustrates the process of brewing," Stutrud says. "The brewing process dictated the layout, but Peter's design enhanced this functional point of view."

T.E. Ibberson of Hopkins, Minnesota, a firm specializing in food manufacturing facilities, provided the engineering for Summit's brewery. Nerb & Co., a small, family business in Freising, Bavaria, is responsible for the brewing process controls and automation that keep this state-of-the-art

THE BREWERY HAS A CURRENT CAPACITY OF 70,000 BARRELS, WITH ROOM TO GROW ULTIMATELY TO 300,000 BARRELS WITH THE INSTALLATION OF NEW FERMENTATION AND STORAGE TANKS AND AN ADDITION TO THE CURRENT STRUCTURE.

brewery running smoothly with consistent quality.

Beyond the bricks and mortar, the real evidence of Summit's success is in the beer the company produces. Summit now produces seven different beers, including several seasonal brews such as Summit Heimertingen Maibock, a very malty, pale bock beer brewed with German lager yeast, which is available in April and May; and Summit Winter Ale, a darker brew with a spicy taste, which debuts in November each year.

"People tend to think that beer is just a beverage similar to soda—you do some mixing and all of a sudden you have beer," Stutrud says. "It's really much more complex and challenging."

The process starts by heating crushed barley or wheat malt in pure, filtered water. The sweet liquid that results is called wort. The wort is boiled and hops are added. After separating the spent hops from the liquid, yeast is added for fermentation. Finally, the beer is filtered for clarity. For those interested in observing the process first-hand, Summit offers brewery tours three times a week, which include a tasting afterwards.

A Bright Future

Since moving into its spacious new quarters in December 1998, Summit has continued to grow and prosper—despite some analysts' predictions at the time that the popularity of small, regional breweries like Summit had begun to wane.

Summit is currently the second-largest brewery in the state after Minnesota Brewing Co., and the eighth-largest supplier of beer in Minnesota. Outside of Minnesota, Summit distributes its products between Chicago in the east and Bismarck in the west. Eventually, Stutrud says, Summit brews will be available in a 10-state area in the upper Midwest.

Stutrud has no doubt that Summit will continue to compete successfully. The new brewery has a current capacity of 70,000 barrels, with room to grow ultimately to 300,000 barrels with the installation of new fermentation and

storage tanks and an addition to the current structure.

"It will probably take us another 15 to 20 years to get to that level," Stutrud says. "This year, we're on track to do 48,000 barrels," he says, noting that sales growth in the last five years has averaged 25 per-

cent a year. Shareholders in the private company number approximately 300, and the brewery employs some 40 people. "In spite of moving to the new facility and taking that risk, Summit Brewing Company is doing very well," says Stutrud.

KNOWN FOR AUTHENTIC ITALIAN FOOD PREPARED WITH THE UTMOST care and freshest ingredients, Ristorante Luci and its sibling restaurant, Luci Ancora, have become institutions in the Twin Cities. Owned and operated by the Smith family, these restaurants provide an inviting neighborhood feel and good value to their customers.

The restaurants are named for Lucille Smith, who, with her husband, Al, opened Ristorante Luci as a retirement hobby in 1988. Today, their children are involved in the daily operation—Daniela is the chef at Ristorante Luci, Stephen is executive chef, and Maria is involved in general operations. Anna, another daughter, has been in charge of the front of the house until recently and still manages the wine program.

All of the children have waited tables or contributed their particular skills to the business at some point. During the first few years, everyone in the Smith family pitched in. The wait staff consisted of other people they knew from school and around the neighborhood.

The Kohler family, longtime friends of the Smiths', also continue to be an integral part of the operation. Jim Kohler is chef at Luci Ancora, Kris Kohler Hennessy is head of the baking department, and Kelly Kohler is a cook for both restaurants.

Family matriarch Lucille Smith is of Italian descent, has long been recognized as an exceptional cook, and gives final approval to all menu items. "No menu gets published in this place without Lucille's permission," says Al Smith.

While the menus are creative and the dishes are drawn from many regions of Italy, they are also simple

RISTORANTE LUCI, LOCATED IN AN OLDER BRICK BUILDING IN ST. PAUL, SEATS JUST 38 PEOPLE AND HAS A TINY KITCHEN, MAKING IT A TRUE APPROXIMATION OF AN ITALIAN TRATTORIA.

and straightforward. "Simple is always better," Lucille Smith says. "We do simple things, but we do them extremely well."

A REAL TRATTORIA IN ST. PAUL

Ristorante Luci was the result of three ingredients: love of Italian cuisine, the pleasure of gathering with friends and family around a table loaded with good food and wine, and just plain good timing.

The Smith family spent 11 years in Italy while Al was assigned there as part of his job for 3M. "That is where we really became fond of the food," Lucille Smith says. "We recognized that we were going to eat that way wherever we were."

When they returned to St. Paul in 1972, the Smiths found plenty of good Italian-American restaurants in the Twin Cities, but none that served the food that Italians in Italy preferred. "We thought at that time that if someone opened a real Italian trattoria, it would be a nice addition to the city," Al Smith says.

Smith continued working at 3M until 1988, enjoying his wife's cooking and their relaxed, warm family gatherings around the dinner table. Upon his retirement, Al and Lucille decided to open the restaurant they had envisioned, Ristorante Luci.

"Our goal was to make a real Italian trattoria in St. Paul," Al Smith says, recalling the small, friendly restaurants throughout Italy where the food is sophisticated while the atmosphere is relaxed and neighborly. The other requirements were that the restaurant should be small and located in the area of St. Paul where the family lives.

Ristorante Luci, located in an older brick building in St. Paul, seats just 38 people and has a tiny kitchen, making it a true approximation of an Italian trattoria.

"This food isn't easy to do for a lot of people," Al Smith says. "Even 38 seats requires a lot of hard work but is also a lot of fun. It really caught on." The pasta is freshly made on-site, as are the desserts.

WHILE THE MENUS ARE CREATIVE AND THE DISHES ARE DRAWN FROM MANY REGIONS OF ITALY, THEY ARE ALSO SIMPLE AND STRAIGHTFORWARD.

"People liked the feel of the restaurant," Lucille Smith says. "Like they do in Italy, people sit close to each other. It's a noncorporate feel."

INNOVATION AND EXPANSION

After nearly a decade of critical acclaim, full reservation lists, and competition from a growing number of Italian restaurants in the Twin Cities, the Smiths decided to expand their restaurant offerings. Luci Ancora opened in a totally renovated space across from Ristorante Luci. It serves both lunch and dinner, seats 70 people, and is more airy and spacious for guests, as well as for the kitchen staff.

The menus reflect what is in season, so the ingredients are always fresh. In the summer, a local farmer provides the produce for the restaurant, using organic growing methods. "With the ingredients, quality is everything," Al Smith says. "We use small suppliers who grow things the way we want them."

Anna Smith monitors the wine program, which includes a variety of vineyards that extend beyond Italy. Every several months, the restaurants offer a wine dinner that includes a full Italian meal with the traditional seven or eight courses and different wines accompanying each dish.

"Italy is a very important resource for us," Al Smith says. He and Lucille, as well as other members of the family, travel to Italy at least once a year and sometimes as often as three times a year to expand their repertoire of recipes and wines. The Smiths are contemplating a kitchen staff exchange program in which some Italian friends who have restaurants in Italy will come to St. Paul to offer new ideas in the kitchen and cooking demonstrations for the public.

FROM HOBBY TO BUSINESS

The Smith family's retirement hobby has become a successful business, but Al says this kind of hobby lasts a lifetime.

"We have to continue to improve every day and continue to make improvements forever," Al Smith says. "You never really arrive; you just keep getting closer to your goal. Our goal is to provide the best Italian food and best value in the Twin Cities. The people who really benefit from this philosophy are our customers."

OWNED AND OPERATED BY THE SMITH FAMILY, THESE RESTAURANTS PROVIDE AN INVITING NEIGHBORHOOD FEEL AND GOOD VALUE TO THEIR CUSTOMERS.

LUCI ANCORA OPENED IN A TOTALLY RENOVATED SPACE ACROSS FROM RISTORANTE LUCI. IT SERVES BOTH LUNCH AND DINNER, SEATS 70 PEOPLE, AND IS MORE AIRY AND SPACIOUS FOR GUESTS, AS WELL AS FOR THE KITCHEN STAFF.

LONG CHENG, INC.

WHEN 19-YEAR-OLD MUACHUA YANG ARRIVED IN ST. PAUL FROM Thailand in October 1979, Long Cheng, Inc. was a dream to this Hmong man, who wanted to own his own business. Shortly after he arrived, his brother took him to a farm on the outskirts of the city, where the farmer would slaughter animals for the growing

Asian immigrant population in the area and sell the animals at a cheaper rate than at the city grocery stores.

Yang remembers the difficulty in transporting the animal. "It was very inconvenient, especially in the winter. You'd have to clean it at home. I thought to myself that someone should start something for the Hmong people."

And that was the seed of the idea that eventually became Long Cheng, Yang's custom slaughterhouse and retail meat market now located five miles from St. Paul.

Long Cheng is the name of the village in Laos where the CIA based its Secret War operations in the late 1960s and early 1970s. The Hmong people, who are primarily farmers in the highlands of Laos, helped the Americans in Laos during the Vietnam War. "Americans should not forget about Long Cheng," Yang says, explaining why he named his business after this village.

JUST SHORT OF HIS TENTH ANNIVERSARY OF IMMIGRATING TO THE UNITED STATES, MUACHUA YANG AND HIS WIFE, TIA, OPENED LONG CHENG, INC. 5 MILES FROM ST. PAUL.

LONG CHENG IS AN IMPORTANT EMPLOYER IN THE LOCAL HMONG COMMUNITY. THE COMPANY CURRENTLY EMPLOYS 16 TO SLAUGHTER PIGS AND CHICKENS.

A DREAM COMES TRUE

Before Yang was to realize his dream, he studied accounting in college and later worked two jobs to earn the capital to start his business. He was sure his idea for a slaughterhouse near town would

fill a niche in the Hmong and greater Asian immigrant community, but he had difficulty convincing others to loan him any money.

So he worked 15 hours a day as a job developer for Lutheran Social Services and as an English as a Second Language (ESL) coordinator for an area Lutheran church. After he married, his wife, too, went to work full-time to help raise the capital to start the business. Just short of his

tenth anniversary of immigrating to this country, Yang opened his business, Long Cheng, in August 1989.

"New immigrants can't adjust right away to the new culture," Yang explains. "It takes decades to become accustomed to cooking styles."

Asians, like many Africans and Hispanics, follow different customs when it comes to eating meat. For instance, others like to cook the meat, fat, and skin together. Asians prefer medium-sized pigs with less fat than those that provide the pork sold in supermarkets in this country. Asians also like non-broiler chickens, which take longer to grow and are more like barnyard or free-range birds.

Not only does Long Cheng cater to immigrants' tastes, but it also saves them almost 50 percent of what they would pay in the grocery stores. "A family can purchase a whole pig for $100 to $130," Yang says. "We cut down on the middlemen [who make meat more expensive to buy in the supermarket], and can save some money for families," he says. "Then they can use the money for kids' needs and help keep the family values together."

A LOCAL EMPLOYER

Long Cheng, Inc. also is an important employer in the Hmong
community in the city. "We can
employ more non-English-speaking
or hard-to-place workers," Yang
says. "We, in the process, take
them off the welfare system and
help save the government money."

Currently, Long Cheng employs
16 people to slaughter pigs and
chickens. Yang hopes to expand
the business, moving into a more
spacious building and adding sheep
and goats to his product list as,
well as becoming a supplier to
stores frequented by the immigrant
population. This year, Long Cheng
grossed some $2.4 million in sales.

"This business was designed to
serve the 16,000 Hmong people here
in 1989," he says. "Now, there are
approximately 60,000 people, plus
Africans, Middle Eastern people,
and Central Americans; all of these

groups number more than 100,000
in the Twin Cities area now."

Eventually, Yang would like to
secure a contract to produce related
or nonrelated products, such as
beef jerky or dry bones for dogs, as
a way to expand his core business
and employ more people in the
Hmong community.

"We could offer cheaper labor
for assembly line or industrial jobs,"
he says. "Long Cheng could create
different branches and be a role
model in the community. The
Hmong need more business."

REMEMBERING HIS COUNTRYMEN

Besides helping the local
Hmong community through
his business, Yang also wants to
help the Hmong in Northern Laos,
Thailand, and Vietnam, where they
are minorities and do not receive
much help or support from the

governments of those countries.

"For our people to survive there,
they need more industrial jobs to
work and earn money," he says. "If
any company wants to be there, I
would definitely recommend relocating into a Hmong town. Put
your company in a Hmong town.
It would be inexpensive for the
company. The Hmong are very
honest people and willing to learn.
They are very fast learners."

Yang says government policies
in the countries where the Hmong
live have taken away the farmland
and the livelihood the people have
known for generations.

"I need my people to have a life
there with other work besides farming," Yang says. "They struggle and
face tough issues there. With a business opportunity like this one, I can
make a difference in their lives. In
offering them an alternative, I can
give them hope."

NRG Energy, Inc.

*I*N LITTLE MORE THAN A DECADE, NRG ENERGY, INC. HAS BECOME the world's fifth-largest independent power producer (IPP). "Our phenomenal success has come from staying focused on our vision of becoming a leading global generation company with a top-three position in our core markets—a vision that we have achieved by sticking with

strategies that work," says David H. Peterson, chairman, president, and CEO. "These strategies include leveraging our presence in existing markets, forming alliances with other energy leaders to increase our asset base, and developing future core markets that meet NRG's investment criteria."

NRG's operations, which span the globe, include independent power production and cogeneration facilities, power marketing, district heating and cooling production, thermal energy production and transmission facilities, and resource recovery facilities. The company has become known as an expert in overhauling and reactivating inefficient operations and restructuring financially distressed projects.

Landfill gas generation, refuse-derived fuel, steam transmission facilities, and district heating and cooling operations generated NRG's early success. Today, these projects continue to be an important part of the NRG portfolio and have differentiated the company as an IPP experienced in diverse fuels and alternative strategies. In Minnesota, where the company is headquartered, resource recovery and thermal energy operations are the building blocks of NRG.

RESOURCE RECOVERY

*N*RG is among the largest producers of refuse-derived fuel in the United States. The company's Minnesota resource recovery facilities in Elk River and Newport process more than 870,000 tons of municipal solid waste yearly, with more than 90 percent recycled or recovered for use as fuel in power plants.

"Resource recovery is part of the solution to solid waste management in Minnesota," says Doug Walker, managing director, Resource Recovery. "Recycling is an answer. We believe in reusing it if we can."

NRG's Resource Recovery operation was established in 1987 to work with local governments to develop an alternative fuel source through reusing solid waste. Over the years, a visionary partnership was developed, according to Walker, and to this day, NRG's Resource Recovery facilities work with Ramsey County—as well as 13 other counties and 30 cities in the state—to provide refuse-derived fuel and recyclables.

Without Resource Recovery, this unusable material would otherwise be deposited in landfills, producing no additional benefits for Minnesota's citizens. "It is a

NRG ENERGY, INC.—THE WORLD'S FIFTH-LARGEST INDEPENDENT POWER PRODUCER—HAS BECOME KNOWN AS AN EXPERT IN OVERHAULING AND REACTIVATING INEFFICIENT OPERATIONS AND RESTRUCTURING FINANCIALLY DISTRESSED PROJECTS.

long-term solution that not only protects the environment, but also protects the health and welfare of the citizens," Walker says.

The ferrous metals and other recyclables produced by Resource Recovery are sold to local businesses, while the materials used for fuel are packed into trucks and shipped to Great River Energy's Elk River waste-to-energy power station. Here, the refuse-derived fuel is used in specially modified boilers to create high-pressure steam that turns turbine generators. The electricity generated can serve some 25,000 homes.

At NRG's Elk River Resource Recovery facility and the company's Newport Resource Recovery Facility approximately 1,500 tons of solid waste are processed each day, with more than 90 percent being recovered as refuse-derived fuel or recyclables. The refuse-derived fuel produced at NRG's facilities is used in three power plants, which generate more than 70 megawatts of electricity from what otherwise would have been deposited in a landfill.

NRG THERMAL CORPORATION

NRG Thermal Corporation is a wholly owned subsidiary of NRG Energy, Inc. The company is an experienced owner/operator of thermal energy businesses, serving a variety of customers who require high reliability.

Since its beginnings in the early 1980s as Norenco, selling steam to industrial customers from Northern States Power plants, NRG Thermal Corporation has become the second-largest owner and operator

of thermal heating and cooling systems in the United States.

A rapidly growing company, NRG Thermal Corporation doubled its size in 1999, significantly strengthening its position in the United States. Just as it has in 1998, 1999, and 2000, NRG Thermal is targeted to grow 20 percent every year. In Minnesota, its businesses include the Minneapolis Energy Center, Hennepin County Energy Center, WashCo, and Highbridge Station.

In 1990, NRG Thermal assumed operations of the Hennepin County Energy Center, which serves the Hennepin County Medical Center and the Metrodome sports center in downtown Minneapolis. Sales total approximately 425 million pounds of steam per year.

The Minneapolis Energy Center, which NRG acquired in 1993, serves some 93 steam customers and 38 cooling customers. In its five plants, the Minneapolis Energy Center produces 1.2 million pounds of steam per hour and 35,000 tons

of chilled water. Sales total approximately 1.2 billion pounds of steam per year.

NRG Thermal's steam line transmission businesses include WashCo, which processes steam for Andersen Corporation and the Minnesota Correctional Facility. WashCo, which has been in service since 1986, has sales totaling 380 million pounds of steam each year. And in St. Paul, the Highbridge Station along the Mississippi River serves the Rock-Tenn Paper Company, also in St. Paul, through a five-mile, closed-loop, high-pressure steam line. Sales at the Highbridge Station, which began service in 1983, are at 2.4 million pounds of steam per year.

In each of its operations, NRG Energy, Inc. keeps its strategic vision in mind. Says Peterson, "In the future, we will continue to apply the same formula for success—a strong strategic approach to growth combined with the efforts of great, talented people."

THE OPERATIONS OF NRG ENERGY, INC. INCLUDE INDEPENDENT POWER PRODUCTION AND COGENERATION FACILITIES, POWER MARKETING, DISTRICT HEATING AND COOLING PRODUCTION, THERMAL ENERGY PRODUCTION AND TRANSMISSION FACILITIES, AND RESOURCE RECOVERY.

SITMA USA, INC.

THE PRODUCTS SITMA USA, INC. MANUFACTURES MAY BE TRANSPARENT to most people. But the magazine wrapped in plastic that arrives in the mail; the shrink-wrapped package of thank-you notes, gift wrap, or stickers; or the phone books bundled together with plastic were probably neatly wrapped by Sitma equipment. ▨ The international

company, which has been in St. Paul since 1990 and in the United States since 1980, is a world-class leader in the manufacturing of innovative packaging systems. "We have 88 percent of the market share for the commercial printing market in North America," says Peter Butikis, managing director and CEO for Sitma USA. "Last year we did approximately $85 million

in sales worldwide, which is significant for a privately held company. Business is great worldwide and the possibilities for expansion are very promising."

SISTERLY RELATIONSHIP

The world headquarters and manufacturing facilities for Sitma USA are located in Spilamberto, Italy, halfway between

Bologna and Modena, in the country's north central region. This area is known worldwide for its packaging machinery industry. At Sitma's 175,000-square-foot facility in Italy, 225 dedicated craftsmen research, design, and manufacture flexible, durable, problem-solving equipment and systems for almost any packaging application imaginable.

Founded in Italy in 1965, Sitma expanded to Melun, France, in 1979. A year later, Sitma crossed the Atlantic Ocean and settled in Hackensack, where Sitma USA began.

In the late 1980s, the St. Paul connection was established when then St. Paul Mayor Jim Scheibel began touting the Sister City program. The first Sister City relationship for St. Paul was with Modena. At the time, Sitma was looking for a new location for its U.S. branch. After several trips back and forth between St. Paul and Modena, Sitma officials decided to settle

"BUSINESS IS GREAT WORLDWIDE AND THE POSSIBILITIES FOR EXPANSION ARE VERY PROMISING," SAYS PETER BUTIKIS, MANAGING DIRECTOR AND CEO OF SITMA USA, INC. (TOP).

SITMA USA, INC. IS A WORLD-CLASS LEADER IN THE MANUFACTURING OF INNOVATIVE PACKAGING SYSTEMS (BOTTOM).

their company in St. Paul in 1990. By 1998, Sitma USA had already completed an 18,000-square-foot addition to its 15,000-square-foot facility to keep up with demand for its packaging equipment.

Today, in Sitma's U.S. headquarters just behind the Minnesota State Capitol, 16 employees work assembling the machines, training operators, and filling orders for parts for the North American market.

The Sister City relationship still exists, as evidenced by the publication of a glossy coffee-table book in Italian and English profiling Modena and St. Paul. Also, at the company's annual party, each employee is given a gift of a kilo of parmesan cheese and a bottle of balsamic vinegar, for which Spilamberto is famous.

SERVING THE CUSTOMER

The machines that Sitma manufactures can perform tasks such as wrapping in paper or poly at a variety of speeds, and will accept a complete range of product sizes. Other machine components can insert, label, address, stack, and bundle. Because the line is made up of a series of machines with each one doing a different task, Sitma's products can be customized to fit the specific needs of each customer.

"We've created some unique applications," Butikis says. "Every machine is customized to the end user. We can even design and build a specific machine for a customer, and then it becomes standard."

Many newspapers, like *The Washington Post*, use Sitma USA's machines to collate and insert advertising or to wrap the paper in plastic. With new recommendations from the U.S. Postal Service, many publications now are sent in plastic to protect them as they go through the mail, which creates even greater demand for Sitma's products.

With the growing market, Sitma USA has begun to do assembly work in St. Paul to improve the time to market, Butikis says. The parts manufactured in Italy are shipped to St. Paul, where the final assembly of the machinery takes place.

Customer service is key to Sitma's success, Butikis says. The company offers in-house or on-site operator training, and has engineers on call for troubleshooting and service information. The customer service department is accessible 24 hours a day, seven days a week for spare parts.

"We keep $750,000 in inventories of spare parts to serve the customer," Butikis says. "We're not going to get people's business unless we serve the customer."

Sitma USA's customer-oriented philosophy will ensure the company's position as a world-class leader in the manufacturing of innovative packaging systems for decades to come.

TODAY, IN SITMA'S U.S. HEADQUARTERS, JUST BEHIND THE MINNESOTA STATE CAPITOL IN ST. PAUL, 16 EMPLOYEES WORK ASSEMBLING THE MACHINES, TRAINING OPERATORS, AND FILLING ORDERS FOR PARTS FOR THE NORTH AMERICAN MARKET.

CONNECTING IMAGES, INC., A LEADING INTERACTIVE MULTIMEDIA COMPANY, has been around for the last decade, putting the latest and best technology to work for its clients. ▨ Connecting Images has gained a wealth of experience and perspective during the continual evolution of interactive multimedia. The company has honed a process that is based on a thorough understanding of its clients' business models.

"We are not out to impress everyone with the whiz-bang stuff," says Vicky Frank, president. "We provide strong interface design and effective communication strategies to produce results more enduring than the latest bells and whistles."

Connecting Images prides itself on not bandying the latest high-tech lingo, such as e-business, e-support, and e-tailing. As one of Connecting Images' recent advertisements states: "E schmee. It's just plain business! Connecting Images has been providing interactive and multimedia business solutions for almost a decade. We're not about the latest tricks and gimmicks. We're about planning, designing, and developing Web sites that fit your business."

THE WEB REVOLUTION

In 1991, few, if any, businesses had heard of the Internet or thought about what a Web site might do for their company. The Internet's expanding accessibility to the general public has launched a revolution.

"The Web has taken our world and opened it up," Frank says. "Much of the hype is about the Web being the first new advertising medium to come along in 50 years. What we are experiencing is that the Web may be one of the first new ways of doing business to come along in 50 years.

"Using the Web to reach a specific audience is unlike using a brochure, billboard, kiosk, or video, and requires new ways of thinking about marketing," Frank adds. Connecting Images' specialty is using the Web to maximize businesses' benefits.

"The Web opens up the opportunity to do business in new ways and in places where you never did business before," Frank says.

Frank offers an example of a well-established bank that hired Connecting Images to create its Web site. During the development process, Connecting Images gathered pertinent information about their clients' needs and goals, and identified a new business opportunity for the bank to expand its customer base. It emerged that the bank could serve a previously untapped audience by delivering its products and services on-line more profitably than off-line banking could provide.

"The Web was an opportunity for the bank to do business in a new and better way," Frank says.

Connecting Images' clients include Fortune 500/1000 companies like 3M, Cray Research, Honeywell, and American Express, as well as small- to medium-sized businesses, city government, and organizations in the arts, education, and entertainment communities.

Connecting Images guides clients through the maze of technology choices to the end product. While refraining from overwhelming clients with the depth of its technological abilities, Connecting Images certainly has the resources to complete the most technologically advanced projects. Clients are looking for simplicity for the user, but at the same time, a level of complexity that calls for database-driven, customizable content, e-commerce, or Shockwave- and Flash-enhanced text, animation, audio, and video.

The company also creates CD-ROMs for interactive kiosks, laptops, desktops, or CD-ROM/Web hybrids for use in sales presentations, marketing, training and

IN THE HEART OF THE BEAST—
MINNEAPOLIS, MINNESOTA

3M LITTMANN STETHOSCOPES—
WORLDWIDE

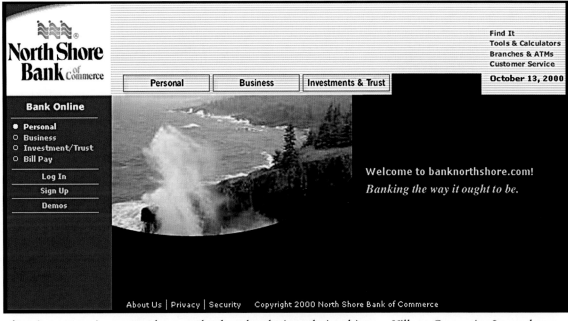

education, entertainment, and speaker support—or for supporting other communications material. And since content development is often crucial to success, Connecting Images offers skilled copy writing, editing, animation, print, video, and audio development, database design, and digital imaging. Connecting Images also provides consulting services and seminars to help companies take advantage of the best that multimedia has to offer.

ROOTED IN ST. PAUL

Since its establishment in St. Paul, Connecting Images has developed enduring relationships with its clients and the community, such as the Saint Paul Riverfront Corporation and the Ordway Center for the Performing Arts. One of Connecting Images' more lighthearted projects for the City of St. Paul was the creation of a Web site and Snoopy map for Peanuts on Parade, a unique, communitywide public art tribute to cartoonist Charles Schulz, a former St. Paul resident. This event gained international attention and received more than a million hits on its Web site.

Located in downtown St. Paul in historic Lowertown's Cyber Village, Connecting Images began with several "refugees from the corporate world, who were looking for something different and to make an impact," Frank says. Through the years, Connecting Images has grown to approximately 20 employees, with plans for continued expansion.

The company reinvests its profits into the business, creating stability and greater profitability, and sustaining its prized longevity. With a truly innovative approach to doing business and a commitment to quality work, Connecting Images is a dynamic leader in its industry.

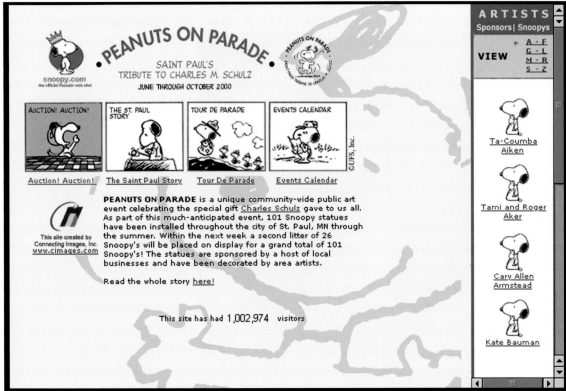

SHAVLIK TECHNOLOGIES

S HAVLIK TECHNOLOGIES IS A PREMIER INFORMATION TECHNOLOGY (IT) consulting firm that helps businesses achieve a competitive advantage by improving efficiency through the latest technology. ▨ "We help companies utilize what they have already and be more effective with it," says Mark Shavlik, company founder. Shavlik follows

a project from initial wish list through implementation and troubleshooting. The firm anticipates and stays on top of emerging technologies to help businesses plan for future needs, as well.

Shavlik Technologies offers clients a blend of consulting services expertise and actual products that Shavlik engineers have designed in order to meet the special needs of e-businesses. Founded in 1993, the company is unique in St. Paul because it is the city's only 100 percent Microsoft Certified Solution Provider Partner, which allows Shavlik to solve some of its clients' toughest business and technical challenges by customizing the latest Microsoft solutions.

THE REDMOND CONNECTION

S havlik was a senior developer for Microsoft Corporation, and one of the founding members of the Microsoft Windows NT® team. Originally from Wisconsin, he decided to return to the Midwest and launch his own business after five years with Microsoft. Minnesota—and St. Paul, in particular—

impressed Shavlik and his wife, Rebecca, as a good place to raise a family and a good market for the expertise Mark had gained while working at Microsoft.

"We looked at the whole country and picked Minnesota," Shavlik says. "We consider Minnesota one of the best-kept secrets in the country. We have clients from California who come here and say they would consider moving here because they like the attitudes and atmosphere."

At first Shavlik's personal goal was to direct his own career and be independent. For the first three years of his company's existence, rapid growth was not the intention. At the end of the three years, there were four full-time employees, including Shavlik himself; one part-time employee; and a few subcontractors.

In 1997, Shavlik Technologies was recommended to become a Microsoft Certified Solution Provider Partner. At the time, the company was probably the smallest partner Microsoft had in the country, Shavlik says. Being a partner means that Microsoft helps develop the business while the partner helps Microsoft expand the scope of its business.

Shavlik Technologies has seen phenomenal growth and positions itself for further expansion. By the end of 1997, there were 23 employees

MARK SHAVLIK, FOUNDER OF SHAVLIK TECHNOLOGIES, CONSIDERS MINNESOTA ONE OF THE COUNTRY'S BEST-KEPT SECRETS BECAUSE OF ITS QUALITY WORKFORCE, ENVIRONMENT, AND ATMOSPHERE.

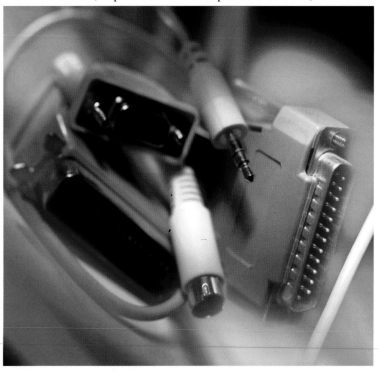

FOUNDED IN 1993, THE COMPANY IS A PREMIER INFORMATION TECHNOLOGY CONSULTING FIRM THAT HELPS BUSINESSES ACHIEVE A COMPETITIVE ADVANTAGE BY IMPROVING EFFICIENCY THROUGH THE LATEST TECHNOLOGY.

at Shavlik Technologies. Today, the company employs more than 50 people and has started to build a sales force to lengthen the firm's reach. Within five years, Shavlik anticipates having a staff of 200 people nationwide, with a sales force of 15.

"It is imperative for us to expand geographically beyond Minnesota to continue to grow," Shavlik says. One-third of the company's revenue is from West Coast-based clients, with some international business being conducted in Canada and Great Britain.

"This brings more development to the St. Paul area," Shavlik says. "The workforce is good; the environment is good. We like bringing projects here."

ON THE CUTTING EDGE

With experienced IT employees at a premium, Shavlik Technologies has worked hard to create an inviting corporate culture that attracts and retains the best and the brightest in the business. Simple things such as free soft drinks and a birthday gift certificate make the workplace environment more pleasant. But Shavlik Technologies also offers substantial benefits. Everyone has all the necessary tools to do his or her job in the most efficient and best possible way, which means portable computers, car allowances, and cell phones. Everyone is offered the opportunity of employee ownership in the company, and currently most of the staff are owners.

To encourage new employees to pass the necessary Microsoft certification exams promptly after beginning work at Shavlik, the company offers a DVD player to anyone who passes the exams within six months of their starting date, as well as providing the textbooks needed. Shavlik Technologies has

also developed its own internal training program, Shavlik Technologies Advanced Resources (STAR), to keep employees up to date.

Becoming a Shavlik employee—and, as such, privy to these benefits—is not an easy task, however. Job candidates must pass a difficult interview process designed to uncover how quickly they can solve and analyze a situation.

Despite Shavlik Technologies' rapid growth, the small company feel remains. "No one gets lost," Shavlik says. "We want to make sure it's to their advantage to stay with us for the long term."

*F*OHN DILLINGER DANCED HERE, MA BARKER FREQUENTED THE PLACE, and legend has it that Al Capone himself visited. The seven interconnecting caves now known as the Wabasha Street Caves are not natural caverns. Rather, the towering holes in the Mississippi River bluffs were formed in the mid-1800s when the fine, white sandstone was mined for its silica.

Once a fancy St. Paul nightclub, the caves have been restored to their 1930s charm, and today serve as a hot spot for receptions, swing dancing, and historic tours.

When the properties were first purchased in 1992 by Stephen and Donna Bremer, the city was about to condemn the site. Stephen Bremer was looking for a location for his commercial construction company, Bremer Construction, and felt the location was ideal. The company acts as a general contractor specializing in tenant finishes and new or re-modeled restaurant space. Paul Friesz and Jerry Holmberg keep the firm's jobs on schedule with the help of Tom O'Shaughnessy, Kevin Arrigoni, and Will Bremer. They use some of the unfinished cave space for storage of equipment and tools for the construction company.

Developing a Unique Event Center

As the caves' history became known and the cleanup began, Friesz and the Bremer Construction crew began diligently working to restore the caverns back to their 1930s splendor. Caterers got word of the project and started to book events in the caves. From there, the business has mushroomed into the Wabasha Street Caves. Currently, the caves are a thriving event center with a fountain and a fireplace. Thursday nights are reserved for swing dancing to the sounds of 16- to 22-piece big bands on stage, and the stage is home to an annual theater performance. The rest of the time is available for private lease. Special events such as corporate parties or wedding receptions are handled by the Bremers' oldest daughter, Heather Radloff.

In 1995, the Bremers began doing a historic cave tour, featuring stories of mushroom farming, gangsters, and ghosts. Shortly thereafter, the Bremers purchased Down in History, home of the Saint Paul Gangster Tour, a tour company offering costumed character guides who give visitors a historical snapshot of pertinent events. The Bremers' cave tours began with the Saint Paul Gangster Tour, and now include Mill City Mobs, Victorian, Literary, and Rivers & Roots tours, plus seasonal offerings. Deborah Frethem, tour manager and historian, continually works to improve current presentations and develop new tours.

New Team Members, New Developments

The Bremers recently added Grumpy Steve's Coffee in a vacant building on the premises. Stephanie Bremer is managing the enterprise, and offers souvenirs for both Grumpy Steve's and the Down in History tours, as well as some cave items and Scandinavian trolls. Serving coffee, pastries, and sandwiches, Stephanie Bremer and Mike Feidt make the atmosphere a comfortable and friendly place to enjoy a fresh cup of Grumpy Steve's coffee.

Another valued team member, Norm Campbell, sees to the behind-the-scenes work and keeps everything from construction to coffee running smoothly. As proprietors of the seven interconnecting caves, the Bremers owe the growth of this interesting and historic site to their multitalented employees. As the team of employees, family, and friends develops, so too will the Wabasha Street Caves' unique contribution to the St. Paul area.

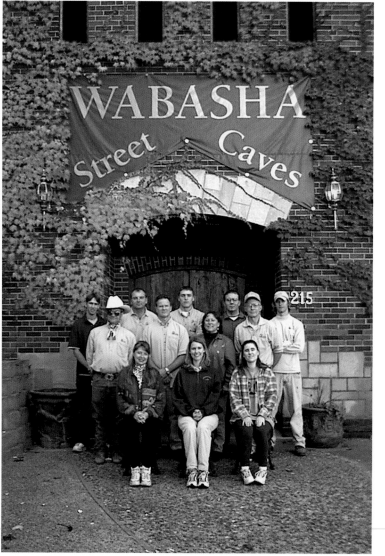

AS THE TEAM OF EMPLOYEES, FAMILY, AND FRIENDS DEVELOPS, SO TOO WILL THE WABASHA STREET CAVES' UNIQUE CONTRIBUTION TO THE ST. PAUL AREA.

Bluestem Systems, Inc. is a professional service company delivering business and technology solutions for public and private Fortune 1000 organizations, government agencies, and innovative start-up companies. The talented team of Bluestem application developers, network engineers, project managers, technical architects, and business consultants help

businesses meet today's most complex information technology challenges by delivering real solutions for real business needs.

The company was formed in 1995 when five individuals, all of whom had been employed by large corporations, decided to start their own company. They wanted to be different from other professional service firms by "delivering technologically superior solutions that drive behavior and achieve clients' goals," says Peter Hager, vice president and cofounder.

Bluestem Systems' measure of success for all solutions is return on investment. From e-business and knowledge management to security, infrastructure, and network management, the company's passion is delivering high-value, quick return on investments.

Bluestem's first office was in CyberVillage, located in the historic Lowertown area of downtown St.

Paul. This village was planned as an incubation area for technological companies of all types. The founders were taken in by the rich history and old-world charm that the area has to offer.

Since the incorporation of the company in 1995, Bluestem has grown to a staff of approximately 60 people. The significant growth in staff prompted relocation to the elegant and historic St. Paul University Club building in the heart of downtown St. Paul.

In addition to outstanding employment growth, the company has seen remarkable growth in revenue. For employees, that means a generous benefits package that rivals any Fortune 500 company. In the St. Paul community, the firm's growth in revenue means financial support and a willing, enthusiastic volunteer force. "We believe in investing in our employees and our community," says Hager. In addition to numerous

company contributions, Bluestem employees volunteer their time at a variety of youth and educational organizations.

Bluestem Systems is a unique and true value service business. "We're a blend of business and technology savvy," says Hager. "We're a project-based company specializing in adding value by delivering solutions our clients actually use."

Industry research has shown that fewer than 30 percent of all information technology (IT) projects are actually implemented. "At Bluestem, nearly 100 percent of the projects the firm manages are fully implemented," says Hager.

With many notable clients and a strong portfolio of services, Bluestem is well positioned for continued growth. "We believe in pragmatic, stable growth," Hager says. "We're committed to our employees, our clients, and the community. We're here for the long term."

Bluestem Systems, Inc. is a professional service company delivering business and technology solutions for public and private Fortune 1000 organizations, government agencies, and innovative start-up companies. The company's executive management team is comprised of its cofounders Bruce Lach (center), president; Bill Prairie (top left), sales; Peter Hager (bottom left), marketing; Blaine Nelson (top right), technology; and Barry Pederson (bottom right), architecture.

FOUNDED IN 1999 AS THE ONLY NATIONAL LAW FIRM WITH ITS HEADquarters in St. Paul, Larson • King, LLP has unlimited national and international resources available to successfully resolve the most important and challenging problems facing individual and corporate clients. ▣ "The world is experiencing vast change at an unprecedented pace, so many

of the problems are unprecedented," says Dale I. Larson, one of the experienced team leaders of the law firm. "The legal challenges and crisis situations confronting clients today are evolving—often becoming more troublesome in scope and magnitude. We believe the firm is properly positioned to help clients meet these changing needs."

At Larson • King, clients have a highly trained and experienced group of attorneys acting as a nucleus directing and successfully resolving major litigation. What sets this firm apart is its ability to select and work with both national and international, legal and non-legal talent in specialized areas to bring the best resources to each case and its unusual experience on all sides of major controversies. Larson • King regularly coordinates the activities of hundreds of selected attorneys throughout the country.

"Rather than limiting our clients or ourselves to our own array of talent, we strongly believe we can offer them unparalleled service by engaging and working with specific talents from other top firms from time to time," says partner Lawrence R. King.

law profession's brightest innovators and creative thinkers. In addition to St. Paul, Larson • King also has offices in Boston, Miami, and San Francisco.

"Dale Larson and the team at Larson • King have the unique and rare talents shared by the best trial lawyers in the country. They are setting new standards and creating a law firm with a new vision," says James Brosnahan, a prominent trial lawyer and member of California's Trial Lawyers Hall of Fame.

For decades, the attorneys at Larson • King have successfully served clients facing mass tort and complex litigation. They have been involved in many of the high-profile natural, environmental, and product catastrophes litigated over the past 30 years. Examples include breast implant litigation, asbestos litigation, Dalkon Shield litigation, the Times Beach Dioxin disaster in

Missouri, the MGM Grand fire in Las Vegas, the Teton Dam collapse in Idaho, and the Union Carbide disaster in Bhopal, India.

Larson • King attorneys also have experience handling atypical litigation matters, such as presenting employment cases to administrative law judges, handling reinsurance arbitrations, or successfully defending claims through tribal court systems.

Larson • King's unique approach produces extraordinary client service. Not only do clients in any part of the country have the best attorneys and legal resources available working on their problem, they are also assured of constant teamwork and communication among everyone involved. Larson • King brings unexcelled courtroom experience and a fresh perspective to the changing realities of the current legal landscape.

THE ONLY NATIONAL LAW FIRM WITH ITS HEADQUARTERS IN ST. PAUL, LARSON • KING, LLP BRINGS UNEXCELLED COURTROOM EXPERIENCE AND A FRESH PERSPECTIVE TO THE CHANGING REALITIES OF THE CURRENT LEGAL LANDSCAPE.

A SOLID CORE

The core group of more than 40 trial attorneys at Larson • King offers an immediate depth of experience. The founding members are skilled courtroom advocates, and are regarded as some of the

BEGINNING AS A SMALL PUBLISHER OF LOCAL NEWSPAPERS IN THE 1930S, Towery Publishing, Inc. today produces a wide range of community-oriented materials, including books (Urban Tapestry Series), business directories, magazines, and Internet publications. Building on its long heritage of excellence, the company has become global in scope, with

cities from San Diego to Sydney represented by Towery products. In all its endeavors, this Memphis-based company strives to be synonymous with service, utility, and quality.

A DIVERSITY OF COMMUNITY-BASED PRODUCTS

Over the years, Towery has become the largest producer of published materials for North American chambers of commerce. From membership directories that enhance business-to-business communication to visitor and relocation guides tailored to reflect the unique qualities of the communities they cover, the company's chamber-oriented materials offer compre-

hensive information on dozens of topics, including housing, education, leisure activities, health care, and local government.

In 1998, the company acquired Cincinnati-based Target Marketing, an established provider of detailed city street maps to more than 200 chambers of commerce throughout the United States and Canada. Now a division of Towery, Target offers full-color maps that include local landmarks and points of interest, such as recreational parks, shopping centers, golf courses, schools, industrial parks, city and county limits, subdivision names, public buildings, and even block numbers on most streets.

In 1990, Towery launched the Urban Tapestry Series, an award-

winning collection of oversized, hardbound photojournals detailing the people, history, culture, environment, and commerce of various metropolitan areas. These coffee-table books highlight a community through three basic elements: an introductory essay by a noted local individual, an exquisite collection of four-color photographs, and profiles of the companies and organizations that animate the area's business life.

To date, more than 80 Urban Tapestry Series editions have been published in cities around the world, from New York to Vancouver to Sydney. Authors of the books' introductory essays include former U.S. President Gerald Ford (Grand Rapids), former Alberta Premier Peter Lougheed (Calgary), CBS anchor Dan Rather (Austin), ABC anchor Hugh Downs (Phoenix), best-selling mystery author Robert B. Parker (Boston), American Movie Classics host Nick Clooney (Cincinnati), Senator Richard Lugar (Indianapolis), and Challenger Center founder June Scobee Rodgers (Chattanooga).

To maintain hands-on quality in all of its periodicals and books, Towery has long used the latest production methods available. The company was the first production environment in the United States to combine desktop publishing with color separations and image scanning to produce finished film suitable for burning plates for four-color printing. Today, Towery relies on state-of-the-art digital prepress services to produce more than 8,000 pages each year, containing more than 30,000 high-quality color images.

AN INTERNET PIONEER

By combining its long-standing expertise in community-oriented published materials with advanced production capabilities, a global sales force, and extensive data management capabilities, Towery

TOWERY PUBLISHING, INC. PRESIDENT AND CEO J. ROBERT TOWERY HAS EXPANDED THE BUSINESS HIS PARENTS STARTED IN THE 1930S TO INCLUDE A GROWING ARRAY OF TRADITIONAL AND ELECTRONIC PUBLISHED MATERIALS, AS WELL AS INTERNET AND MULTIMEDIA SERVICES, THAT ARE MARKETED LOCALLY, NATIONALLY, AND INTERNATIONALLY.

are often produced in conjunction with chambers of commerce and other business organizations.

Despite the decades of change, Towery himself follows a long-standing family philosophy of unmatched service and unflinching quality. That approach extends throughout the entire organization to include more than 120 employees at the Memphis headquarters, another 80 located in Northern Kentucky outside Cincinnati, and more than 40 sales, marketing, and editorial staff traveling to and working in a growing list of client cities. All of its products, and more information about the company, are featured on the Internet at www.towery.com.

In summing up his company's steady growth, Towery restates the essential formula that has driven the business since its first pages were published: "The creative energies of our staff drive us toward innovation and invention. Our people make the highest possible demands on themselves, so I know that our future is secure if the ingredients for success remain a focus on service and quality."

has emerged as a significant provider of Internet-based city information. In keeping with its overall focus on community resources, the company's Internet efforts represent a natural step in the evolution of the business.

The primary product lines within the Internet division are the introCity™ sites. Towery's introCity sites introduce newcomers, visitors, and longtime residents to every facet of a particular community, while simultaneously placing the local chamber of commerce at the forefront of the city's Internet activity. The sites include newcomer information, calendars, photos, citywide business listings with everything from nightlife to shopping to family fun, and on-line maps pinpointing the exact location of businesses, schools, attractions, and much more.

DECADES OF PUBLISHING EXPERTISE

In 1972, current President and CEO J. Robert Towery succeeded his parents in managing the printing and publishing business they had founded nearly four decades earlier. Soon thereafter, he expanded the scope of the company's published materials to include *Memphis* magazine and other successful regional

and national publications. In 1985, after selling its locally focused assets, Towery began the trajectory on which it continues today, creating community-oriented materials that

SAINT PAUL

LIBRARY OF CONGRESS CATALOGING-IN-PUBLICATION DATA

Molitor, Paul, 1956-
  Saint Paul : home for all seasons / [Paul Molitor] ; introduction by Paul Molitor ; art
direction by Robert Shatzer.
    p. cm. — (Urban tapestry series)
  Includes index.
  ISBN 1-881096-88-2 (pbk.)
    1. Saint Paul (Minn.)—Civilization. 2. Saint Paul (Minn.)—Pictorial works. 3. Saint
Paul (Minn.)—Economic conditions. 4. Business enterprises—Minnesota—Saint Paul. I.
Title. II. Series.

F614.S4 M74 2001
977.6'581—dc21   00-066325

TOWERY PUBLISHING, INC., THE TOWERY BUILDING,
1835 UNION AVENUE, MEMPHIS, TN 38104

WWW.TOWERY.COM

PRINTED IN CHINA

Publisher: J. Robert Towery **Executive Publisher:** Jenny
McDowell **National Sales Manager:** Stephen Hung **Market-
ing Director:** Carol Culpepper **Project Directors:** Susan
Adams, Sue Blumberg **Executive Editor:** David B. Dawson
Managing Editor: Lynn Conlee **Senior Editors:** Carlisle
Hacker, Brian L. Johnston **Editors:** Jay Adkins, Rebecca E.
Farabough, Danna M. Greenfield, Sabrina Schroeder
Editor/Caption Writer: Stephen M. Deusner **Editor/
Profile Manager:** Ginny Reeves **Profile Writer:** Elaine
Ellis Stone **Art Director:** Robert Shatzer **Photography
Editor:** Jonathan Postal **Photographic Consultant:** Randy
Johnson **Profile Designers:** Rebekah Barnhardt, Laurie
Beck, Glen Marshall **Production Manager:** Brenda Pattat
Photography Coordinator: Robin Lankford **Production
Assistants:** Robert Barnett, Loretta Lane, Robert Parrish
Digital Color Supervisor: Darin Ipema **Digital Color
Technicians:** Eric Friedl, Brent Salazar, Mark Svetz **Digital
Scanning Technicians:** Zac Ives, Brad Long **Production
Resources Manager:** Dave Dunlap Jr. **Print Coordinator:**
Beverly Timmons

Photographers

Originally from Minneapolis, **Conrad Bloomquist** specializes in scenic, landscape, and nature photography. The owner of Scenic Photo!, a stock photo agency, Bloomquist has been the recipient of numerous awards.

As a freelance photographer, **Amy Jo Clark** specializes in travel and wildlife images. She has exhibited in nine juried art shows and has been recognized with three best-of-show awards, in addition to many other technical and artistic honors.

A graduate of the University of Minnesota School of Journalism, **Scott Cohen** is a freelance photographer based in the Twin Cities area. Cohen works for the *St. Paul Pioneer Press*.

As a veteran travel writer and photographer, **Lee Foster** has seen his work has been published in major travel magazines and newspapers. He maintains a stock library that features images of more than 250 destinations worldwide.

Before coming to the *St. Paul Pioneer Press* in 1999, **Jim Gehrz** was a photographer at the *Worthington Daily Globe* in Worthington, Minnesota, where he was named Minnesota Photographer of the Year in 1985. He was named Photographer of the Year six times in Wisconsin while at the *Journal Sentinel*, and one of his photographs from Super Bowl XXXII was honored as the 1997 Pro Football Hall of Fame Photograph of the Year.

A photographer for the *St. Paul Pioneer Press*, **Scott Goihl** has worked as an agricultural economist for the federal government and as a video photographer in Missoula, Montana.

Janet Hostetter is a staff photographer for the *St. Paul Pioneer Press*, where she has worked for 15 years.

An award-winning amateur photographer from Grimes, Iowa, **John Jentsch** specializes in cities, people, and travel photography. His most recent assignments have taken him from the Indiana Sand Caves of northeast Iowa to the Badlands of South Dakota.

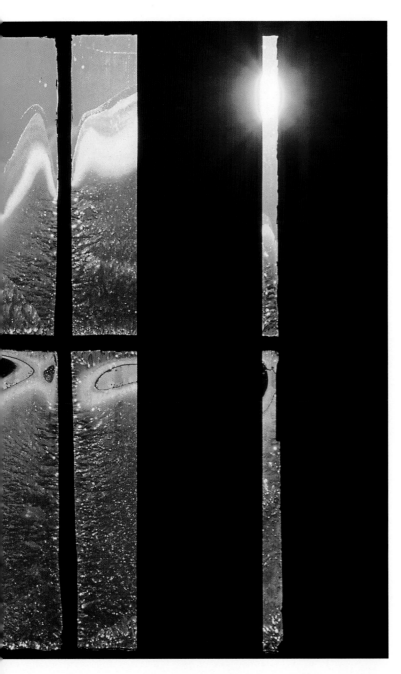

nesota Twins winning the World Series and has been a photographer for the *St. Paul Pioneer Press* since 1983.

Specializing in nature photography, **CHRIS POLYDOROFF** has worked as a staff photographer with the *St. Paul Pioneer Press* since 1987.

Born in London, **AMIRALI RAISSNIA** has lived in Minneapolis since 1997 and is a graduate of the University of Minnesota.

Born and raised in Northern Minnesota, **JOE ROSSI** started working in newspapers in 1976 and has been associated with the *St. Paul Pioneer Press* since 1983.

STEVE SCHNEIDER has photographed people and places on location in and around the Saint Paul area. His clients include the Dayton-Hudson Corporation, Luther Seminary, University of Minnesota, Children's Cancer Research Fund, Musicland, Ruttger's Sugar Lake Lodge, and many others.

Specializing in travel and nature photography, **KAY SHAW** is the owner of Kay Shaw Photography and is widely published in books, magazines, newspapers, and calendars. Originally from Minneapolis, she has traveled to 29 countries and most of the 50 states.

Since 1997, **SAINT-PAUL.COM** has been an established city guide for Saint Paul as a unique, on-line informational reference. Saint-Paul.com is owned and operated by M.R. Danielson Advertising, an agency that designs, develops, and produces integrated print campaigns and new media.

With photographs and essays appearing in publications such as *National Wildlife*, *National Geographic*, *Sports Illustrated*, and *Outdoor Photographer*, **RICHARD HAMILTON SMITH** supports the causes of the Nature Conservancy, Wilderness Society, Wilderness Inquiry, and the National Arbor Day Foundation. Currently, he is exploring the motion and multiple exposure effects on his already-established signatures of color, light, and design.

Listed in *America Artists of Renown*, *Who's Who in Photography*, and *Who's Who in the World*, **CURTIS B. STAHR** has photographed life in each of the contiguous United States and has walked with his camera across Canada from ocean to ocean. He has exhibited in 32 juried/invitation art shows and 16 one-man shows, and has received 11 purchase awards.

Having started her career as a photographer at the *Minnesota Daily*, **DAWN VILLELLA** has worked for newspapers in Duluth, Pittsburgh, and other cities. She has spent the last four years working part-time for the *St. Paul Pioneer Press*, stringing for the *Associated Press*, and freelancing for both local and national publications. Her work has appeared in *USA Today*, *Time*, and other publications.

STEVE WEWERKA specializes in people, portraiture, and candid image photography. As the owner of Steve Wewerka Photography, he has images in several major publications such as *Life*, *Time*, and *Sports Illustrated*.

Other contributors include **GEOLIMAGERY**, **TIM A. HINTZ**, the **MINNESOTA OPERA**, *St. Paul Pioneer Press*, and **SCIENCE MUSEUM OF MINNESOTA**. For information about photographers with images appearing in *Saint Paul: Home for All Seasons*, please contact **TOWERY PUBLISHING, INC.**

During his 14 years at the *St. Paul Pioneer Press*, **RICHARD MARSHALL** has been a staff photographer and photo editor. A native of Detroit, he has worked at newspapers in Michigan and New York State.

After beginning his journalism career in the U.S. Army, **JOE ODEN** arrived at the *St. Paul Pioneer Press* in 1970 and has worked there ever since.

PHOTOPHILE, established in San Diego in 1967, has more than 1 million color images on file, culled from more than 85 contributing local and international photographers. Subjects range from images of Southern California to adventure sports, wildlife and underwater scenes, business, industry, people, science and research, health and medicine, and travel photography. Included on Photophile's client list are American Express, *Guest Informant*, Franklin Stoorza, and Princess Cruises.

A Minnesota native, **JEAN PIERI** has covered subjects ranging from AIDS in rural Minnesota to famine in Africa. She covered the Min-

SAINT PAUL

INDEX OF PROFILES